Digital Cameras
For Beginners

By Web Wise Seniors, Inc.
An education program for beginning computer users

Web Wise Seniors, Inc.
305 Woodstock Rd.
Eastlake, Ohio 44095
www.WebWiseSeniors.com

Copyright

Trademarks

Windows is a registered trademark of Microsoft. All other brand names and product names used in this book are trademarks, registered trademarks, or trade names of their respective holders. Web Wise Seniors is not associated with Microsoft or any other product or vendor mentioned in this book.

Limits of Liability/Disclaimer or Warranty

Web Wise Seniors, Inc. has used its best efforts in preparing this book. WWS makes no representation or warranties with respect to the accuracy or completeness of the contents of this book, and specifically disclaims any implied warranties or merchantability or fitness for any particular purpose, and shall in no event be liable for any loss of profit or any other commercial damage, including but not limited to special, incidental, consequential, or other damages.

Sales Inquiries

For sales inquiries and special prices for bulk quantities, please call toll free (866) 232-7032.

Introduction

"The best computer class I have ever taken!" and "I never knew that computers could be explained so well!" are frequent comments made by Web Wise Senior students. Since 2000, Web Wise Seniors has successfully taught thousands of beginning computer users.   Now, for the first time, the same teaching methods successful in Web Wise Seniors courses are found in this easy to understand book.

This book is not a reference for computers. It is a learning guide for people of any age who are unfamiliar with computers, but especially designed for seniors who want to be skilled computer users. It is like having a private instructor by your side as you walk through the basics of computer use with your book. This book is full of common questions, asked in real classes by beginners, with easy to follow answers that have already helped thousands.

Reading explanations and definitions will only get you so far. You need to actually use the computer to learn to use it, and this book will help you do just that. It will help you get started using the computer by walking you through basic skills step-by-step while answering your "whys" and "whats" along the way.

Web Wise Seniors teaches basic computer classes every day. WWS has seen what works, what doesn't work, and what beginners want to know first hand.

About the Authors

Web Wise Seniors is a company dedicated to teaching basic computer skills to individuals over the age of 50. Since 2000, Web Wise Seniors has filled over 22,000 classroom seats throughout Ohio, and has quickly become a premier computer education company for mature adults in the Midwest.

Classes have been designed for seniors by seniors and continually updated with the feedback of its students. By becoming an interactive part of the senior community and working closely with senior organizations throughout Ohio, Web Wise Seniors has been able to develop a unique teaching style and curriculum that has met with overwhelming success.

Since 2000, over 98% of Web Wise Seniors students said they would recommend the program to their friends and family. 100% of affiliated teaching locations have been happy to work with the WWS program and out of a 4 point scale, WWS received on average a 3.77 rating in student satisfaction.*

The same dedication and love of teaching that has made the WWS program so successful in the classroom is available for you in the pages of this book. Readers will find this book full of examples, illustrations, and easy to follow directions. This is a teaching guide, not just a manual or reference book.

*Student satisfaction as collected through WWS classes and events (2000 – 2006).

About this Book

Digital Cameras for Beginners is designed to be read in order. Readers should begin with page one and continue through the book as if they were actually taking a computer course. The sections all relate and build upon each other.

Readers should keep a digital camera or computer close at hand while reading **Digital Cameras for Beginners**. We recommend you read through an entire section and then go back and try the steps outlined in the section.

Keep a pen or pencil handy too. Take notes and highlight any sections that you feel are personally important. This is your computer book and the more personal references you make within its pages, the better this course will work for you.

Above all, please enjoy **Digital Cameras for Beginners**. Read at your own pace and keep at it. You'll be a digital camera wiz before you know it!

Meet Larry

Larry is the Web Wise Seniors mascot. He will be found throughout the pages of this book, helping you to "get the bugs out". Larry has been helping beginning computer users for over two years now. He runs the WWS help desk on www.WebWiseSeniors.com and often makes guest appearances in WWS publications.

In his spare time, Larry enjoys searching the Internet, e-mailing friends, and belly dancing.

Acknowledgements

We would like to thank the thousands of students that have challenged our computer instructors' minds in class. Your countless, and sometimes off-the-wall, questions and constructive feedback have made us better teachers. Without you, this book would not have been possible. Thank you!

We would also like to thank our family members for their insight, feedback, and support.

Credits

Author
Mark Weiker

Book Design and Production
Mark Weiker
Steve Pelton

Proof Reading
Mary Pelton
Jean Pelton

Clip Art
Microsoft 2003 Clip Art Gallery

Screen Shots
Microsoft Windows XP

Table of Contents

Table of Contents

Table of Contents

Table of Contents

Table of Contents

Chapter 7: Using Your Digital Camera **47**

Chapter 8: Taking Pictures & Using Your Digital Camera **51**

Table of Contents

Chapter 9: Digital Camera Functions and Menus

Chapter 10: Using External Memory

Table of Contents

Table of Contents

Table of Contents

Table of Contents

Chapter 15: Working in the My Pictures Folder

Table of Contents

Table of Contents

Table of Contents

Table of Contents

Table of Contents

Chapter 1

An Introduction to Digital Cameras

What You Will Learn in This Chapter
- ✓ What is a digital camera?
- ✓ Do I need to know how to use a computer to use a digital camera?
- ✓ Digital Cameras vs. Traditional Cameras

Section 1: What is a Digital Camera?

A digital camera, much like a traditional camera, is a device that allows individuals to take and store pictures. As you know, traditional cameras store images on film, to be later developed into larger pictures by photo processing labs. Digital cameras instantly store pictures digitally in memory, eliminating the need to send them to a lab for processing.

At-Home Film Processing
A digital camera gives you the opportunity to process your film at home using your own computer. Instead of having to take the film to a developer, you have control. You can take pictures, delete, crop, change picture size, add color, and save your pictures on a computer or CD.

How it Works
Digital cameras usually have either internal or external memory (which you will learn about soon). A digital camera stores pictures much like a computer stores files. With digital cameras, the files can be transferred to a computer and either viewed through the computer monitor (television-like device attached to the computer) or printed on an attached printer.

Section 2: Do I Need to Know How to Use a Computer to Use a Digital Camera?

It is very helpful to have at least a basic working knowledge of computers to use a digital camera effectively. Computer knowledge is beneficial because:

1. Typically, pictures are transferred to computers from digital cameras.
2. Transferring pictures to a computer may be the only way to save them permanently.
3. Transferring pictures to a computer gives you the ability to edit pictures.
4. Transferring pictures to a computer gives you the ability to email pictures.
5. Transferring pictures to a computer allows you to save and resave pictures for generations, without fading or discoloration.

It *IS* possible to use a digital camera without knowing how to use a computer, but it certainly helps to know some computer basics before you try to perform tasks such as picture editing and emailing.

NOTE: Some digital camera manufacturers give you the option to send your pictures from your digital camera directly to a printer. In this case, the printer and digital camera are usually made by the same manufacturer. For instance, the printer and digital camera would both be manufactured by Kodak.

Having a digital camera that works directly with a printer eliminates the need to use a computer for printing. However, emailing, saving, organizing, and editing are tasks that cannot be accomplished without a computer. As you will see in the following sections, these are all important tasks and big benefits to using a digital camera.

If you are new to a computer and to digital cameras, it is possible to learn to use both your digital camera and your computer at the same time, although it may be a little more of a challenge.

<u>Chapter 2</u>

The Digital Difference

What You Will Learn in This Chapter:
- ✓ Why go digital?
- ✓ Benefits of Traditional cameras
- ✓ Drawbacks of Traditional cameras
- ✓ Benefits of Digital cameras
- ✓ Drawbacks of Digital cameras

Section 3: Digital Cameras vs. Traditional Film Cameras

Your first question may be, "Why should I use a digital camera if my old camera works just fine?" This is a very reasonable query, especially if you are proficient with taking and developing pictures using, for example, a 35 millimeter camera. In addition, you may be resisting the purchase of a new digital camera due to the cost factor.

There are certainly benefits and drawbacks of working with both types of cameras, but you'll find that digital cameras have an overwhelming number of benefits compared to traditional film cameras. Generally speaking, here are the pros and cons of both:

Traditional Camera Benefits
- Relatively inexpensive
- Already-learned process of taking pictures and developing film
- Disposable-type cameras are convenient
- Good picture quality
- No computer necessary

Traditional Camera Drawbacks
- Trip to purchase film
- Trip to have film developed
- Film developers see all pictures, no privacy
- Loss of pictures due to camera malfunction
- Loss of pictures due to operator error
- Requirement to purchase all pictures, regardless of quality
- Delay while pictures are developed

- Uncertainty of the outcome of a taken picture, no "preview"
- Uncertainty of what pictures have been taken or are on the film
- Pictures are only on paper, no electronic files
- Pictures can't be emailed or used on a computer
- Traditional cameras are becoming less available in retail stores
- Older photos can become discolored or faded over time
- Making copies of pictures may be difficult or expensive

NOTE: With traditional cameras, film must be processed by a third party. With a digital camera and a computer, you can do it yourself, for FREE!

Digital Camera Benefits
- Operation is similar to a traditional camera
- Photos can be viewed instantly (with LCD, picture preview)
- Unwanted photos may be deleted immediately
- Limited operator error (with LCD, picture preview)
- Photos may be edited, items/people removed, pictures cropped, red eye reduced, text and picture captions added
- Pictures can be saved as files and used on a computer
- Pictures can be emailed
- No trip to purchase film
- No trip, wait, or cost for film development
- Privacy from others seeing your pictures
- Knowledge of exactly what pictures have been taken recently
- Copies of pictures made at no cost
- Electronic files of pictures do not lose color or fade
- Pictures can be stored on a computer (unloaded) allowing you to refill the digital camera memory with new pictures

NOTE: Digital cameras give you the ability to email pictures. Emailing pictures allows you to send pictures to anyone worldwide for FREE!

Digital Camera Drawbacks
- May need to become computer proficient
- May need to have computer access
- Using a digital camera may be unfamiliar and becoming proficient may take time and experience
- May need to spend a significant amount of money on batteries
- Some types of cameras limit the number of pictures that can be taken
- Initial purchase may be expensive, depending upon the features you select

NOTE: Digital cameras can use a lot of batteries, which adds to the cost of operating a digital camera.

Chapter 3

Selecting a Digital Camera

What You Will Learn in This Chapter:
✓ Choosing a digital camera
✓ Deciding what you want to do with a digital camera

Section 4: Choosing a Digital Camera That's Right for You

What Do You Want to Do With the Camera?

It is very important to determine what you want to accomplish with a digital camera before purchasing one. This may seem logical, but often purchases are made blindly, with no regard to the user's intentions.

You don't want to hastily buy a digital camera simply because everyone else has one, or because you feel that you're falling behind the times without one. There is nothing wrong with these incentives to buy. However, if you consider the price range of digital cameras, which spans several hundred dollars, you'll soon realize that it's best to do some research before making your purchase to make certain the camera meets your needs. In this section, we will help you narrow the criteria.

Don't Let the Salesperson be Your Only Guide

It can be a mistake to let the salesperson be your only source of information when purchasing a camera. Although the majority of salespeople are generally interested in what's best for you, it is possible for you to walk out with "way too much camera."

This is especially true if you haven't considered how you intend to use the digital camera. Walking into a retail or camera store without an idea of what you need gives the salesperson the power to artificially create your need. This can make you vulnerable to an over-sale.

On the other hand, you may also walk out with a digital camera that doesn't have the features you need. If you haven't a clue about what you want, it makes it difficult for retail staff to sell you the right camera.

There are many popular motivators to purchase a digital camera. It would be helpful to decide whether you plan to:
- email pictures
- use the digital camera for work
- use it for only special events
- use it daily
- use it for professional photography
- make slideshows
- create flyers with pictures
- place pictures on a website
- create a digital scrapbook.

If you are simply trying to get started in the digital camera age and do not have a specific goal in mind, you should search for (or expect to be led to) a lower-end camera at the lower-end of the price spectrum. Telling the salesman you are a beginner (and that you are looking for a simple, easy-to-use camera) will help the salesman help you find a camera that meets your needs.

If you have yet to purchase a digital camera, please read the remainder of this book before buying a digital camera. This book will help you identify and understand the main differences between digital cameras, allowing you to make more informed decisions as you shop for a digital camera.

Chapter 3: Selecting a Digital Camera

Chapter 4

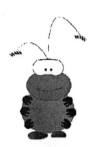

Where Should You Buy a Digital Camera?

What You Will Learn in This Chapter:
- ✓ Where can you buy a digital camera?
- ✓ Advantages of in-store shopping and buying
- ✓ Advantages of online shopping and buying

Section 5: Where Should You Buy a Digital Camera?

Digital cameras may be purchased at almost all electronics stores, office supply stores, and retail superstores. For individuals who are comfortable shopping on the Internet, there are thousands of websites offering digital cameras for sale.

It is important to recognize that there are advantages and disadvantages to both shopping in-store and online. Either way, there are deals to be found!

In-Store Shopping and Buying

If you prefer shopping in-store, or at retail outlets, consider looking for advertised sales by specific retailers. Sales for digital cameras are especially beneficial for digital camera novices. This is true because sales often take place on popular models, which are usually low-to-mid-range priced digital cameras. These digital cameras are usually the easiest for beginners to learn to operate.

Often sales on low-to-mid-range priced digital cameras are meant to lure individuals, who are unsure whether or not to venture into the digital world. This can be a big benefit to someone who is ready to buy and is patient enough to wait for the digital camera with the wanted features and specifications to go on sale.

Salesperson to Aisle 9

One benefit of buying in-store, as opposed to on the Internet, is that you may be able to utilize the advice of the salesperson. As mentioned earlier, the salesperson should not be your sole source of information. However, a salesperson can be a friend when it comes to getting your questions answered.

Please Do Touch and Feel

A second benefit of in-store shopping is that you can touch and feel many digital cameras before buying. In-store displays allow shoppers to see design differences, compare displays, view battery specifications and memory compartments. Combined with your knowledge from this book, and the advice of the salesperson, the in-store "touch and compare" technique can be very educational.

Taking it Back

And lastly, a very important advantage the consumer has when shopping in-store is that returns are easy. If you should decide you don't like the digital camera after one week, perhaps because of some unforeseen feature (or lack of features) you can take it back! This may seem to be a given fact, but returning items when shopping inline isn't as easy.

Section 6: Online Shopping and Buying

Online Shopping and Buying

Shopping online for digital cameras gives the consumer many more choices. Some of the benefits of shopping online include the virtually unlimited selection, comprehensive information, very competitive pricing, and convenience of shopping and purchasing.

Typically, Internet shopping is recommended for consumers who are comfortable with shopping online. As a rule of thumb, if it is your first shopping experience online, you likely do not want to purchase your digital camera online. If you have made purchases in the past, and are confident shopping online, the Internet is a wonderful tool.

Unlimited Selection

The Internet provides a plethora of information for Internet-savvy shoppers. Thousands of websites are published to provide information and to sell digital cameras. The information can be overwhelming however, unless you have a good idea of what you are looking for. With so many models, and so many websites offering digital cameras for sale, it can be difficult to narrow down your search.

Comprehensive Information

Don't think of the Internet as only a resource for buying. The beauty of the Internet is that you can gather lots of free information. Information on the Internet can help you determine what you should pay for a digital camera, what digital cameras may be available in your price range, and perhaps most importantly, what consumers have said about specific digital cameras models.

For individuals who prefer shopping in-store, the Internet can still be a big help. You can use the Internet for researching, to determine what digital camera you want and what you should pay, and then make the purchase in a store.

For consumers who are comfortable buying online, and have the ability to find information effectively on the Internet, buying a digital camera on the Internet may be the most convenient way to go. However, understand that it will be difficult (likely impossible) to get live advice on the Internet about which digital camera to choose. Therefore, you may want to purchase online only if you have a good idea of what type of digital camera you want and are sure that you don't need live or up-to-the-minute advice from a professional or a salesperson.

Chapter 5

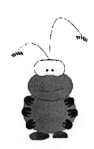

The Big Five Factors To Consider When Choosing a Digital Camera

What You Will Learn in This Chapter:
- ✓ Megapixels
- ✓ Liquid crystal display (LCD)
- ✓ Internal Memory vs. External Memory
- ✓ Will the digital camera work with your computer?
- ✓ Cost of a digital camera

Section 7: Five Factors To Consider When Choosing a Digital Camera

Essential Features to Know

There is quite a spectrum of pricing when it comes to digital cameras. With so many manufacturers, each with so many models, it can be overwhelming to try to make a decision by shopping without a little knowledge.

There are dozens of factors to consider when choosing a digital camera. The choice can be daunting to someone new to the digital camera world. It is easy to get lost in the sea of information about digital cameras because it is difficult to tell which sources are the best, which sources are written for beginners, and which sources are simply advertising pieces by the equipment manufacturer.

In this section, we'll simplify the selection of a digital camera by breaking down the five most important factors: Megapixels, LCD, Memory, "Will the Camera work with My Computer?" and Cost.

Section 8: Megapixels

What is a Pixel?

All pictures taken with a digital camera are made up of thousands of tiny dots which, together with colors and patterns, make up pictures. These tiny dots of color are called pixels. The word PIXEL comes from the combination of

PICture and ELements. Simply stated, these are the basic elements of the picture.

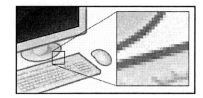

NOTE: Pixels can be seen by magnifying a picture.

The number of pixels in a picture determines the quality of a picture. Increasing the number of pixels-per-inch, also referred to as *ppi*, in a picture will sharpen the picture. Decreasing the number of pixels will decrease the quality of the picture. Pixels may be more evident when pictures are cropped or zoomed.

The pixel is also a common measurement in television resolution. Again, as the number of pixels-per-inch increases, so does the quality of the television picture. Digital cameras are different in that they capture a picture, whereas televisions display a moving picture.

What is a Megapixel?

As televisions are sold based on the quality of the projected picture, digital cameras are sold based on the quality of the captured picture. In other words, digital cameras vary in the amount of pixels contained in the images they capture. Even with the most inexpensive models, digital cameras are typically made to capture millions of pixels per picture. A measure of one million pixels is known as a *megapixel*.

1,000,000 Pixels = 1 Megapixel

How are Megapixels Measured in Digital Cameras?

Rather than list cameras for purchase at 3,000,000 pixels, 4,000,000 pixels, or 5,000,000 pixels, digital cameras are classified as 3 megapixels, 4 megapixels, or 5 megapixels, respectively. Just remember that with an increase in the number of megapixels, there is a direct increase in the quality of picture the digital camera is able to capture. There is also a corresponding increase in price.

There is a large range of megapixels within digital cameras, from approximately 1 megapixel through 8 megapixels. The guide shown on the next page illustrates the limitations based on the megapixel classification of a digital camera.

NOTE: There is no specific megapixel recommendation for beginners or for advanced digital camera users. The number of megapixels needed in a digital camera is based more on the camera's purpose (what you intend to use it for) than on your experience, or inexperience, using a digital camera.

Chapter 5: The Big Five Factors To Consider When Choosing a Digital Camera

Chart for Determining the Needed Number of Megapixels

Number of Megapixels	Emailing Photos	Posting Photos to a Website	Maximum Photo Printing Size (inches) and Quality	Range of pictures able to be stored on a standard size internal memory (16MB)
1.1 MP	✓	✓	4 X 6 with low quality	42-60
2.1 MP	✓	✓	4 X 6 with high quality, 8 X 10 with medium quality	27-42
3.1 MP	✓	✓	8 X 10 with high quality, 11 X 10 with medium quality	16-21
4.4 MP	✓	✓	11 X 10 with high quality, 20 X 30 with medium to low quality	14-23
5.0 MP	✓	✓	20 X 30 with high quality	9-15

Chapter 5: The Big Five Factors To Consider When Choosing a Digital Camera

Megapixels Impact on Emailing Pictures and Posting Pictures to a Webpage.

As the chart indicates, all of the digital cameras listed will take pictures that can be emailed and posted to websites. Both emailing pictures and posting pictures on websites require a relatively low quality picture. Therefore, any new digital camera will give you the picture quality you need to email pictures or to post them to a webpage.

Generally, it is easier to email pictures and to post pictures to a webpage if they are smaller in size (print size and file size) and lower in quality. Even with higher megapixel digital cameras, it is possible to change the settings to take lower megapixel pictures. This may be desirable when pictures are only going to be emailed or posted to a website.

NOTE: A digital camera with a larger number of megapixels will generally allow you to print a bigger picture, while maintaining picture quality.

Megapixels Impact on Picture Size and Printing

The biggest difference in megapixels is in the size of the picture that you'll be able to print. Generally, the higher the megapixels, the bigger the picture can be when you print it. The limitations come in the quality of the printed picture.

As you see on the chart, a 5.0 megapixel digital camera will allow you to print a 20x30 inch picture in high quality. On the other hand, a 1.1 megapixel camera allows you to print a 4x6 inch picture, but it will be a low quality print.

It's important to know that you are able to print ANY size picture on ANY digital camera. However, the quality of the picture decreases as the size of the picture increases, and quality of the picture increases as the size of the picture decreases.

The previous chart simply shows how far a picture can be increased in size and printed without losing quality, as viewed with the naked eye.

NOTE: Although a higher number of megapixels allows you to take better quality pictures, high quality pictures will also take up more room on your digital camera and on your computer.

Megapixels Impact on Picture Storage

Simply stated, better pictures take more room electronically. As the chart indicates, a 5.0 megapixel digital camera may only store up to 13 pictures before a standard size internal memory is filled. (We will discuss other memory options later in the chapter).

Section 9: LCD Screen

Most, but not all digital cameras come with something advertised as an LCD screen. The screen is usually 2x2 inches or less and displays an image of the recently taken picture or pictures stored in a camera's memory. The LCD is typically on the backside of the camera, or on a fold-out panel on the side of the camera.

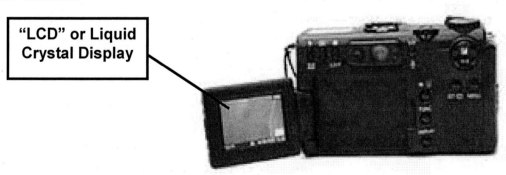

"LCD" or Liquid Crystal Display

Chapter 5: The Big Five Factors To Consider When Choosing a Digital Camera

What does LCD Stand For?

LCD stands for *Liquid Crystal Display* and is similar to the technology used in flat-panel computer monitors and flat televisions. In the case of a camera, the *Display* portion of the screen is a part of the camera.

An LCD displays what you would normally see through the viewfinder

What Does It Do?

The primary benefit of the LCD is that the user can see what the picture looks like immediately after the photo is taken. This lets the person taking the picture decide whether the picture should be kept, deleted, or retaken.

NOTE: An LCD can work as a viewfinder, allowing you to review recently taken pictures.

Another benefit is that the LCD functions as a menu screen you can use to change the digital cameras settings. With an LCD, the digital camera manufacturer incorporates advanced settings because the on-screen menus can be navigated by the user. This allows the manufacturer to include more options than those found in a digital camera without an LCD.

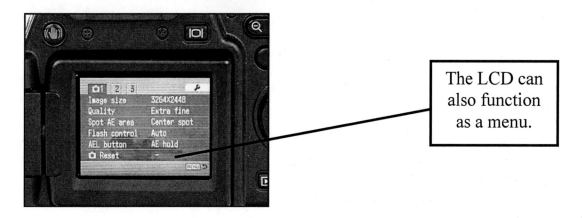

The LCD can also function as a menu.

Some basic digital cameras come without an LCD. A digital camera without an LCD generally offers only basic features. Most camera LCDs act as menu screens for advanced features. Cameras without an LCD do not have advanced features because there isn't enough room to add mechanical knobs for each one.

Is the LCD Important?

As mentioned earlier, one benefit to using a digital camera is the ability to view, delete, and retake pictures immediately after taking a picture. To have this capability, you need an LCD. So, the answer is yes, the LCD is relatively important to achieve the full benefit of digital camera use.

You can purchase a digital camera without an LCD and save money. However, LCDs make digital camera's settings easier to understand, especially for beginners. A digital camera without an LCD uses only symbols on the surface of the camera and on the knobs to mark the camera's settings. Surface symbols alone may be difficult to interpret. Most cameras with an LCD have text labels for their settings directly on the LCD, which help identify the purpose of the functions.

Differences in LCDs

There are two main differences in LCD screens: size and brightness. Both are important in selecting an adequate LCD.

Size of the LCD

In terms of size, choose an LCD that is easy for you to see. Keep in mind that camera price can increase considerably when you increase the size of the LCD.

A large LCD makes pictures easier to see and easier to display to friends and family.

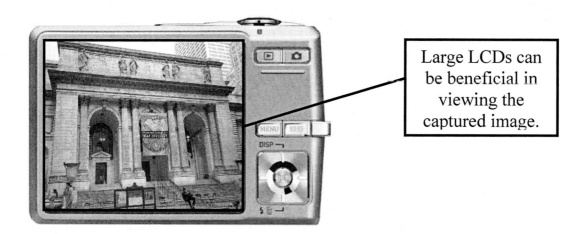

Large LCDs can be beneficial in viewing the captured image.

Brightness of the LCD

Brightness of the LCD is also important to consider before purchase. If the LCD is not bright, it may be difficult to see the LCD in high-light areas, and almost impossible to use outdoors on a sunny day. A large LCD may have little benefit if it is not very bright.

To test the brightness, you may want to ask a salesperson to show you the camera powered up. Compare the brightness of cameras with various prices. If you are purchasing from the Internet, look for ratings and feedback on the brightness of the LCD. There is no standard measure for brightness, however, so user feedback is important.

Section 10: Memory

Digital cameras have memory like computers have memory. Computers store all types of files, including text files, picture files, and video files, to name a few. Digital cameras, on the other hand, store only picture files.

What is Memory in a Digital Camera?
Memory is the storage area in the camera that "holds" the pictures that have been taken. Memory is measured in bytes, which is simply a measure of electronic space.

Think of memory as an empty shopping bag which you fill with items from the mall. Once the space in the shopping bag is used, you either get rid of some items (maybe by unloading them in the car) or don't put any more in the bag.

Similarly, a digital camera's memory will hold only so many pictures. Once full, you must either find a place to put the pictures (like on your computer), delete some pictures, or not put any more pictures on the digital camera. Most people unload the pictures to a computer, saving them, and are then able to use the digital camera to take more pictures.

Why is the Amount of Memory Important for a Digital Camera?
Memory size is important in a digital camera because it is the difference between having a large shopping bag, which has room for lots of items, and a small shopping bag that may have to be unloaded several times.

A digital camera with only a little memory will hold only a small number of images, maybe even as few as 5-10 pictures. In this case, you may attend a wedding or other special event and not be able to take as many pictures as you would like. It would be either impossible, or at least very inconvenient, to unload the pictures to a computer during the wedding to allow you to take additional pictures.

Chapter 5: The Big Five Factors To Consider When Choosing a Digital Camera

Most digital cameras come with a small to medium amount of memory which is inside the digital camera and not removable. This is known as internal memory.

Internal Memory

Internal memory, also known as on-board memory, is in the digital camera when you purchase it. Because internal memory is inside the camera, it cannot be altered. It is impossible to add to the internal memory size to allow you to take more pictures without unloading.

Computers allow tech-savvy users to add memory to their computers; the same is not true with digital cameras. Internal memory cannot be added to a digital camera. To resolve this issue, most digital cameras accept *external memory*.

External Memory

To add memory for more pictures, many digital camera users purchase external memory cards. External memory usually comes in the form of a varying-sized card which is inserted into a slot in the digital camera.

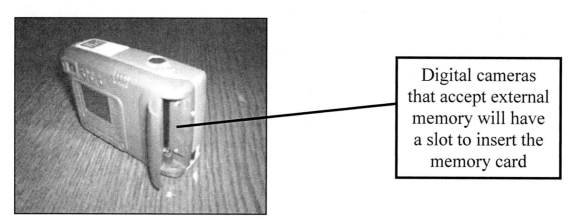

Digital cameras that accept external memory will have a slot to insert the memory card

Memory card sizes vary depending on the manufacturer of the digital camera. External memory cards allow digital camera users to take more pictures than the internal memory will hold.

Below is a chart that illustrates the range of pictures that can be taken given digital camera specifications (megapixels) and amount of external memory.

Chart Illustrating the Range of Pictures That Can Be Taken

Digital Camera Megapixels	Range of Images that fit on a 64MB memory card	Range of Images that fit on a 128MB memory card	Range of Images that fit on a 256MB memory card	Range of Images that fit on a 512MB memory card	Range of Images that fit on a 1GB memory card
4MP	38-57	87-100	166-189	350-400	729-801
5MP	34-45	69-80	141–156	281–315	555–629
6MP	25–36	57–64	111–129	226–259	450–501
8MP	19–23	38–42	72–82	150–168	301–366

This external memory can be referred to as "memory cards," "flash cards," "memory sticks," "external memory cards," or simply "memory."

Specific Types of External Memory

There are different types of external memory used in digital cameras. Here are a few of the differences:

Compact Flash Card – Compact flash cards were the original memory cards used in digital cameras. They are approximately 42mm x 36mm x 3mm. These cards are larger than the others, but also generally less expensive. This is where the term "flash card" was first used, although now the term may apply to any type of external memory.

Chapter 5: The Big Five Factors To Consider When Choosing a Digital Camera

Secure Digital Card – Secure digital cards are the smallest memory card at a size of about 24mm x 32mm and a thickness of 2mm. These cards are about the size of a postage stamp and are currently the most widely used.

Memory Stick – Memory sticks are currently used in only a small percentage of digital cameras. The technology was first widely used by Sony, although other manufacturers have also used this type of memory.

Important Factors to Consider with External Memory

When searching for a digital camera, it is important to determine if external memory can be used, and if so, which type(s) may be used. Below are some other important factors to consider regarding the use of external memory:

- ✓ Does the digital camera accept external memory?
- ✓ What type of external memory is used, i.e. compact flash, secure digital, or memory stick?
- ✓ How much does this type of external memory cost?
- ✓ Does my computer have a "drive" for a memory card? (A drive is a small opening or "slot" that accepts a memory card for picture unloading. It is usually found on the front of the computer tower.)
- ✓ If my computer has a memory drive, does the card size that the computer accepts match the card size that the digital camera accepts?

NOTE: You don't need a memory drive on a computer to use external memory in a digital camera. The pictures stored on external memory can be transferred by leaving the memory in the digital camera and attaching the digital camera directly to the computer. Having a place on the computer to insert an external memory card is simply a more convenient feature.

Some computers have *drives* for external memory cards making it convenient to transfer pictures from your digital camera to your computer.

Section 11: Will the Digital Camera Work with My Computer?

It is important to determine whether or not the digital camera and *software* will work with your current computer. To do this, you'll have to identify the operating system your computer uses and the systems the camera manufacturer states will work with the digital camera.

Finding Specifications on Your Windows Computer

The easiest way to identify your operating system (on a computer running Microsoft Windows) is to watch the computer as it turns on. For approximately five seconds, the computer will flash the name of the operating system your computer uses across the screen. The text that appears on screen will indicate that you have Windows. After the word "Windows" will be letters or numbers indicating the edition you have: "95," "98," "2000," "ME," (for Millennium Edition), or "XP." Write down your operating system and take it with you when you are ready to choose a digital camera.

Below, you will see two Startup screens identifying a computer's operating system. They are Windows 98 and Windows XP, respectively.

 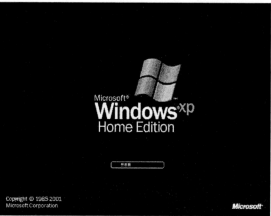

Finding Specifications on a New Digital Camera

To determine the operating systems a digital camera will be compatible with, look on the packaging the digital camera comes in. Typically the specifications are on the back of the package or box that contains the *software* (CD).

Once you find the list of operating systems listed on the box (Note: Windows and Apple have different operating systems,) make sure that your computer's operating system is listed. If your computer's operating system is listed, the software and digital camera will work with your computer.

> Minimum system requirements are listed on the digital camera box.

Software Requirements:
- Windows NT 4.0, with Service Pack 4 (or greater), Windows 2000 Professional, Windows XP
- *Not available for Windows 95/98/ME*
- Internet Explorer 5.0 or higher

Section 12: Cost of the Digital Camera

Certainly, cost is a factor in any purchase. With digital cameras, costs will vary tremendously. Digital cameras may cost as little as $40 or as much as several thousand dollars.

Understanding the first four factors when choosing a digital camera is vital to determining whether or not a price is fair for a digital camera. Only after you have determined how many megapixels you are seeking, what type of LCD you want, how much memory is needed, and which digital camera will work with your computer, can you evaluate digital cameras and price.

Weighing Your Options

To buy a digital camera, first write down the characteristics you want your digital camera to have and then rank them by importance.

Many times, the cost of a digital camera will hinder your search because the characteristics you have determined you want in a digital camera are too expensive. In this case, determine which features are most important to you and be ready to sacrifice the features that are less important.

For example, if you know that you will primarily be using the camera indoors, you may decide that a bright LCD is less important than having a larger amount of memory. Choosing a digital camera with an LCD that is not as sharp, or sacrificing the LCD altogether, may allow you to buy a camera with a higher amount of memory.

The opposite may be true for a consumer with impaired vision who needs a large and sharp LCD. In this case, the consumer may sacrifice some amount of memory or number of megapixels in exchange for a large and sharp LCD that meets the individual's more immediate need.

Chapter 5: The Big Five Factors To Consider When Choosing a Digital Camera

Chapter 6

Zoom, Batteries, and Symbols

What You Will Learn in This Chapter:
- ✓ Zoom
- ✓ Optical vs. Digital Zoom
- ✓ Measuring zoom
- ✓ Selecting and inserting batteries
- ✓ Recognizing common digital camera symbols

Section 13: What is Zoom?

Zoooooom!

Zoom describes a digital camera's ability to move closer to, or farther away from, an object using the camera's lens. On digital cameras, there are two types of zoom: digital and optical.

Zoom is not included in our five most important factors because the standard zoom on a digital camera is sufficient for any beginner. Also, the features described in previous sections are simply more important for beginners.

Zoom can be a confusing topic, especially for first-time digital camera buyers. The most important thing to know is the difference between digital zoom and optical zoom.

Optical Zoom
Optical zoom is a zoom without loss of quality. Most video cameras have optical zoom that allows the videographer to zoom in on objects without losing video quality. Optical zoom on a digital camera is the same. Optical zoom allows you to move closer to the target without sacrificing the quality of the picture itself. Essentially, you can move closer, without being closer. This is the very essence of zoom.

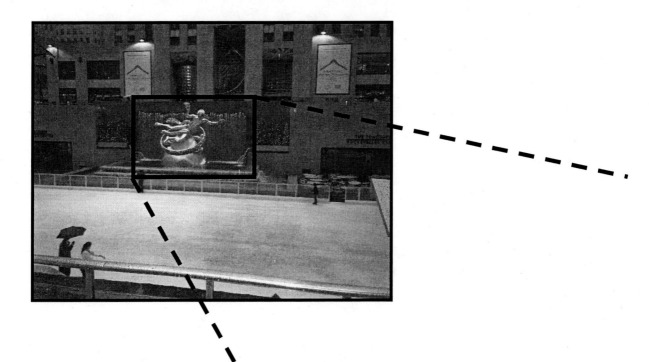

NOTE: Optical zo[om]
quality, much like zoom on a tra[ditional]

You will notice that optical zoom[is]
digital camera with *3X optical z[oom]*
closer without losing picture qua[lity]
still be able to move closer using
utilizing digital zoom means losi[ng]

Digital Zoom

Digital zoom is a feature that engages after optical zoom has been exhausted. Digital zoom continues to zoom closer to the object, but quality IS lost as you continue to zoom closer to the target. Digital zoom is similar to moving closer to an actual photograph or using a magnifier. Quality is lost (the picture becomes more *pixilated* as you continue to zoom).

Digital zoom is listed with a number, just like optical zoom. For instance, 2X digital zoom means that you can zoom in up to 2 times closer, but you will lose picture quality. Digital zoom is in addition to the digital camera's optical zoom distance. Most cameras have both types of zoom, and will be listed side-by-side, such as *3X optical zoom, 2X digital zoom*.

> Digital zoom allows you to zoom closer to an object, but picture quality **will** be lost.

NOTE: Most digital
digital camera is changing from op
usually on the LCD, and may chan
change in the color of the zoom inc
indicate a change from optical to d

As you zoom from Wide angle (W) to Telephoto (T), the zoom bar may change color, indicating that you are switching from optical to digital zoom and, therefore, starting to lose picture quality.

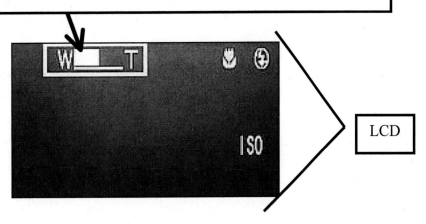

LCD

Section 14: What Type of Batteries Should You Use?

Batteries are a sore point with all electronic devices. In order to best determine the type of battery your digital camera will need, you should consult the camera's user manual. However, if your digital camera does not come with a custom rechargeable battery and charger, it is likely that the digital camera will use AA size batteries.

Typically, there is a door on either the side or the bottom of the digital camera that allows you to remove or insert batteries. It is standard practice for manufacturers to have a chart on the inside of the battery door to illustrate how to insert the batteries. If not, the information will be in the user manual for your digital camera.

The majority of digital cameras use four AA batteries, but that can change depending on your camera's electrical usage. The size of the digital camera's LCD and number of megapixels can add additional need, so be prepared to use anywhere from two to eight AA batteries in a digital camera.

Chapter 6: Zoom, Batteries, and Symbols

Changing the Batteries

As mentioned earlier, one drawback of using a digital camera is that you may have to spend a significant amount of money on batteries. Not only may the digital camera use up to eight AA batteries, it may use them up very quickly. There are four things listed below that you can do to conserve batteries.

Turning Off the LCD When Taking Pictures

This may seem difficult, especially once you grow accustomed to taking and reviewing your pictures on the LCD as soon as you take them. Even reviewing your pictures intermittently, i.e. after 5-10 pictures are taken, will conserve the batteries and help them last up to 50% longer.

Also, most digital cameras will show the picture on the LCD immediately after the picture is taken, even when the LCD is turned off. This is especially helpful because the digital camera will conserve battery power and still allow the user to review the pictures immediately after taking them. The most difficult part of having the LCD turned off is that the person taking pictures must rely on the viewfinder (instead of the LCD) to capture the image. As we will discuss later, this is not always ideal because the image seen through the viewfinder and the LCD don't always coincide.

Reviewing Your Pictures Quickly Using the LCD

When you do review pictures using the LCD, review them quickly. This will limit the time that the LCD is on and using battery power.

Editing and Deleting Pictures on Your Computer, Not on Your Digital Camera

Many digital cameras allow you to edit pictures from the LCD, and all digital cameras allow you to delete pictures from the LCD. Deleting pictures from the LCD is common, but it does utilize the LCD which in turn utilizes battery life. If you have enough storage space on your digital camera to save potentially unwanted pictures, wait to delete them until all pictures are transferred to your computer.

Also, edit pictures on your computer, not on your digital camera. First, the digital camera will have limited editing capabilities. Second, editing pictures on the digital camera itself can be time consuming because the small LCD makes it difficult to see the picture accurately enough to make precise edits.

Lastly, editing pictures on a digital camera uses valuable battery life by overusing the LCD.

Keeping the Digital Camera Off Until You Are Ready to Transfer Pictures to Your Computer

As you'll see later in the book, in order to transfer pictures to a computer, you must turn on the digital camera. To minimize power usage, limit the amount of time the camera is turned on.

To save battery power, leave the digital camera off while you are working on your computer and navigating to the correct location to transfer pictures. Only once you are absolutely ready to make the transfer should you power up your digital camera. And remember, after the pictures are completely transferred, turn off the digital camera. Remembering to turn off the digital camera is often forgotten in the excitement of viewing and editing your new pictures.

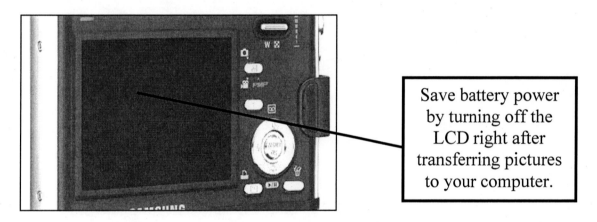

Save battery power by turning off the LCD right after transferring pictures to your computer.

Section 15: Standard Settings and Symbols

This section will explore some of the most common symbols used in the menus of digital cameras. It is important to recognize these modes so that you can use them in appropriate situations.

Many times, the difference between a mediocre and good digital photographer is the ability to use the digital camera features. Recognizing and using these features will allow you to move from good pictures to exceptional pictures.

How Icons are Used on Digital Cameras
Icons, displayed as symbols or pictures or text commands, are a part of the digital camera and allow you to make changes based on the environment, the lighting, and your skill level. The two primary ways the icons can be used are (1) on a manual dial and (2) on the LCD.

Icons on a Manual Dial
Many digital cameras display icons on a manual dial. In this case, you turn the dial to select the desired feature. A manual dial may look like the one below.

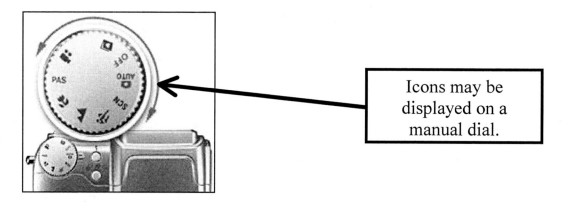

Icons may be displayed on a manual dial.

Icons on a LCD
Some digital cameras have settings listed on the LCD itself. In this case, you must navigate the LCD (with the use of your digital camera's navigation buttons) to select the setting you wish to use. An LCD navigation screen may look similar to the illustrations below.

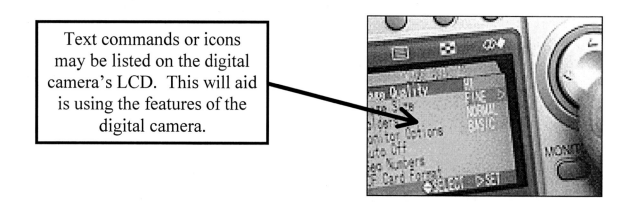

Text commands or icons may be listed on the digital camera's LCD. This will aid is using the features of the digital camera.

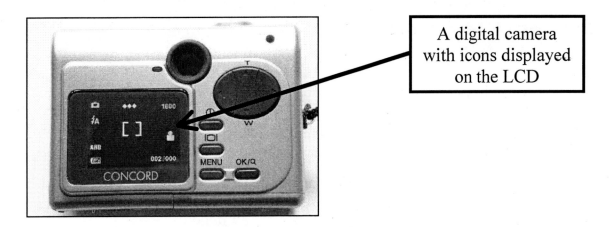

A digital camera with icons displayed on the LCD

List of Common Digital Camera Symbols

Basic Picture Taking Modes

Auto Mode: Auto mode allows you to take pictures without worrying about manually adjusting the camera for specific lighting situations. This "stress free" picture taking mode can be utilized in most situations. This setting is convenient for beginners to use because the camera automatically focuses to the lighting and distance of the target for you.

Manual Mode: Just the opposite of auto mode, manual mode does not automatically focus according to lighting and distance. Some digital cameras do not indicate manual mode with this (or any) symbol. However, anytime you manually adjust your digital camera for lighting or distance, you are working in manual mode.

Macro Mode: Macro mode is best for taking close-up pictures and is represented by a flower icon, which symbolizes nearness. This mode works well when you want to take pictures of people who are posing, for instance at a wedding or social event. Macro mode gives good results and focus for pictures of subjects up to 10-15 feet away from the digital camera.

Macro mode can also be utilized when you are taking pictures of objects to email or post on a website. Macro mode picks up detail well when the object is less than 8 feet away from the digital camera.

Landscape Mode: Landscape mode is the opposite of macro mode and is indicated by an icon symbolizing mountains in the distance. Landscape mode is used to capture a wide picture of an object or target in the distance.

Landscape mode can be used for a large group photo, a boat on water, the horizon, or a cityscape. Landscape mode is not the same as panoramic. Landscape gives you a wider shot by turning the picture sideways; the proportions stay the same. Panoramic view usually limits the height and extends the width, changing the proportions of the image.

Action Mode (aka Sports mode): Action mode is usually represented with a running man icon. Action mode allows you to take pictures with maximum shutter speed to capture people or objects in motion. For instance, you can use action mode during sporting events, to capture a dancing couple, or to photograph moving cars.

Night Mode: Night mode is usually represented by a half moon icon. Night mode increases brightness for pictures by activating the flash. In most digital cameras, the flash engages automatically for all pictures taken in this mode. Night mode uses a slower shutter speed to capture background lights. Night mode can be used for low lit indoor pictures as well.

Movie Mode: Movie mode allows you to take short video clips on your digital camera. Most digital cameras come with this feature. Be aware that recording a short video can use a lot of the digital camera's memory.

Usually, videos are started with a press of the shutter button and ended with a second press of the shutter button. Reviewing a video on the LCD is the same as reviewing a picture on the LCD. When a video is taken, a video review (in motion) can be accessed on the LCD immediately after the video has been taken. Videos can be transferred to the computer in the same manner pictures are transferred.

General Settings Available

Automatic Flash: Automatic flash is typically indicated with an "A" and a lightning bolt icon. This indicates that the digital camera will flash only when needed, based on the amount of natural light in the picture. This setting is convenient, but isn't always consistent. For instance, the flash may fire when you don't want it, and it may not fire when you do want it.

Flash is On: The *flash is on* icon resembles a single lightning bolt. With this setting, the flash will always fire when pictures are taken.

Flash is Off: The *flash is off* icon resembles a single lightning bolt with the "no" symbol around it. With this setting, the flash will never fire when pictures are taken.

Advanced Settings

Reduce Red Eye: The reduce red eye setting is represented by a symbol of a human eye. With this setting, a very short and premature burst of light from the flash forces the subject's pupils to contract, reducing the risk of redeye appearing in the picture.

Countdown Timer: The *countdown timer* setting is represented by a timer icon. With this setting, the digital camera user can set the picture to be taken after a predetermined number of seconds. This allows the person operating the digital camera to be included in the picture.

Digital cameras with multiple time settings may represent the countdown icon with a number which corresponds to the number of seconds before the shutter opens. For example, a ten-second timer may look like the picture to the right.

 10

Date Stamp: The *date stamp* feature is represented by an icon that resembles a stamp. This setting will place the current date on the edge of the picture that is being taken. It's important to make certain the date is set correctly. This step will be outlined in your owner's manual and should be completed before taking any pictures.

Magnify Pictures: *Magnify pictures* is represented by a magnifying glass with a + on it. This allows the digital camera user to zoom in on any picture that has already been taken. This is done while reviewing the pictures on the LCD. This feature does not change the actual size of the picture. It is simply for viewing pictures easily after they have been taken.

Indicator Icons

Battery is OK: Typically represented by a battery icon completely filled in. The *battery is OK* icon is definitely one to pay attention to. When this icon is displayed, you can take pictures without worrying about changing the batteries.

Battery is Near Depletion: *Battery is near depletion* is represented by a semi-filled in battery. At this point, you want to think about how many more pictures you'd like to take and whether you should replace the batteries. Because digital cameras use batteries quickly, you want to plan to replace the batteries when this icon first appears. The next icon that will indicate a change in battery power is the battery is dead icon, so there's not a lot of time to replace the batteries.

Battery is Dead: The *battery is dead* icon is symbolized by an unfilled battery that may be flashing. At this point, most digital cameras will not allow you to take additional pictures until the batteries are replaced. You may also be unable to review pictures or use the LCD when the batteries are very low or dead.

Delete Image from Digital Camera: The *delete image* icon resembles a trash can. This allows you to delete an image from the digital camera's memory. There are two primary times when the delete function is used. The first is directly after the picture is taken. The second is after taking the picture and viewing the image of the picture on the LCD.

<u>Chapter 7</u>

Using Your Digital Camera

What You Will Learn in This Chapter:
- ✓ Understanding the picture taking process
- ✓ Preparing a digital camera for picture taking
- ✓ Turning on a digital camera

Section 16: I Have a Digital Camera, Now What?

Now you are going to learn about how to use a digital camera. Before you begin to take pictures, it will be helpful to understand the entire process from picture taking through organizing pictures on your computer.

Take, Transfer, Edit, Organize

In total, you need to Take, Transfer, Edit, and Organize your pictures. This section will discuss taking pictures. Taking pictures requires the use of the digital camera alone, whereas Transferring, Editing, and Organizing each require an additional component -- the computer. In general, you are going to TAKE the pictures on your digital camera, TRANSFER the pictures to your My Picture folder, EDIT them using Picassa, and then ORGANIZE them in your My Picture folder.

Turning On/Off the Digital Camera

Depending on the type of digital camera you are using, there are a few ways that power may be switched on or off. Power on is typically indicated by a light on the digital camera, sometimes flashing when the digital camera is first powered up.

If the digital camera has an LCD, it may light up to indicate that the power is on. Keep in mind however, that most digital cameras have an option to have the LCD on or off, so it may not be a true indicator of power to the digital camera. It is a better idea to identify which light indicates power, and use the light to recognize whether the digital camera is on or off.

There are typically only three ways to accomplish the task of turning the digital camera on or off. Your digital camera will likely have one of the three features.

Power Button- A simple button is used to power up or power down the digital camera.

Power Button

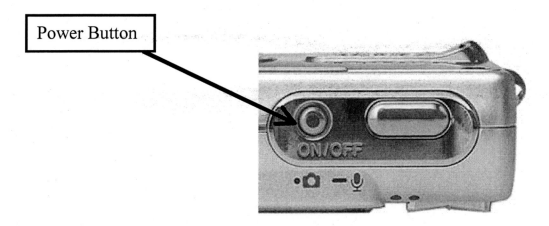

Power Wheel- A wheel may be used to power the digital camera up, power it down, or switch the modes in which the digital camera operates. Typically, there are icons representing "Camera On," "Video On," "Close-Up," "Far Away," and "Camera Off." These icons are identified in the section titled *Standard Settings and Symbols*.

Power Wheel

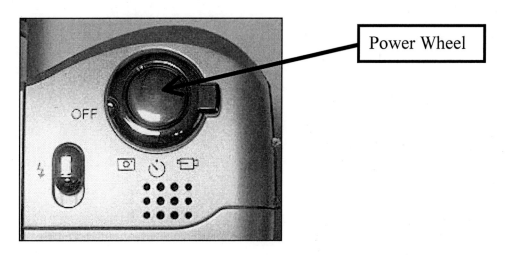

Power Slide- This device simply powers the camera up or down when the user slides a spring-loaded button to the right and then releases the button.

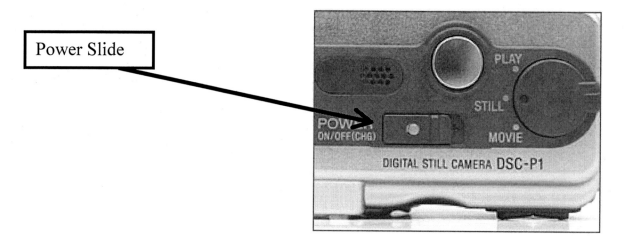

Some point-and-shoot digital cameras, or lower megapixel digital cameras, do not have a power switch. These types of digital cameras operate similar to a standard 35mm camera in that the battery power is used only for the flash and shutter, and only when the shutter button is pressed to snap a picture.

Turning on the Digital Camera: Step-by-Step Instructions
1. **Make sure batteries are in the digital camera.**
2. **Identify and press the power button, wheel, or slide.**
3. **Recognize that power is on by looking at the flashing indicator light next to power button or the LCD.**

Chapter 8

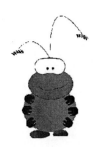

Taking Pictures & Using Your Digital Camera

What You Will Learn in This Chapter:
- ✓ Framing your picture
- ✓ Taking a picture
- ✓ Recognizing shutter lag
- ✓ Reducing shutter lag
- ✓ Using the LCD vs. the Viewfinder

Section 17: Steps to Take a Picture with Any Digital Camera

OK, you're ready to aim and take pictures! Taking pictures with a digital camera is very similar to taking pictures with a traditional film camera.

To get started, you simply frame the object and then snap the shot as you would with any camera. As you'll see, the picture taking process is simplified further with a digital camera because of the LCD.

Framing an Object: Step-by-Step Instructions
1. **Place the target in the circle provided on the digital camera LCD or viewfinder.**
2. **If there are two objects, or multiple people, center the circle between the objects or people.**
3. **Take the picture.**

NOTE: When taking a picture with multiple targets, center the circle on the middle of the group.

NOTE: With three people, as posed above, place the circle on the middle person.

Taking a Picture with Your Digital Camera: Step-by-Step Instructions

1. Make sure the digital camera is powered on.
2. Make sure the flash is charged, if needed ("Flash ready" is usually indicated by a solid light, not blinking. The light is blinking when the flash is charging).
3. Frame your subject in the LCD (or viewfinder if LCD is off).
4. Press the shutter button on top of the digital camera. (The camera adjusts exposure and then takes the picture, which may cause shutter lag, explained below).
5. Review your picture in the LCD on the back of the digital camera.

Taking a Picture with Your Digital Camera: Visual Guide

Step One:
Make sure the digital camera is powered on.

Step Two:
Make sure the flash is charged, if needed.

**Step Three:
Frame your
subject in the
LCD or
viewfinder.**

**Step Four:
Press the shutter
button on top of
the digital
camera.**

**Step Five:
Review your
picture in the
LCD on the back
of the digital
camera.**

Shutter Lag

In the process of taking a picture, you may notice a "lag" between the moment you press the shutter button and when the picture is actually taken. This is known as shutter lag and is common in most digital cameras. During shutter lag, the digital camera is focusing and adjusting for light exposure.

Shutter lag is important to recognize because it may hinder your photography if you are taking action pictures. It also may be difficult to capture a specific moment with shutter lag.

Reducing Shutter Lag

One way to reduce or eliminate shutter lag is to pre-focus your digital camera prior to snapping a picture. To pre-focus, or to eliminate shutter lag:

1. Aim at the picture target with the digital camera.
2. Press the shutter button down only half way and hold in that position.
    - The digital camera will adjust to light, focus, and charge the flash if necessary.
3. Press the shutter button completely to snap the picture when the moment is right.
    - The digital camera will take the picture almost instantly

Shutter lag caused this photographer to miss the target of the picture, the horse.

LCD vs. Viewfinder

There has been some debate among photographers about whether digital picture taking should be done using the LCD or using the viewfinder. There are pros and cons to each method.

Traditional photographers have argued that using the viewfinder remains the best way to align the perfect picture. The reasoning likely stems from early digital camera use, when the LCD did not actually display the picture captured by the digital camera. Many digital cameras only have alignment marks (as shown in the previous section) in the viewfinder. In this case, it may be advantageous to use the viewfinder, and not the LCD, to frame a picture.

More recently, probably due to improved correlation between the LCD image and the actual captured image, there seems to be an increasing number of recommendations to use the LCD for picture taking.

This move toward using the LCD to align pictures may also be due to manufactures adding the picture alignment marks on newer LCD models. These marks help beginners and professionals use the LCD to more accurately align the picture.

Alignment marks may appear on the LCD to help you use the LCD to take pictures.

If You Have It, Use It
It is true that it may be difficult to capture exactly what you want to include using the viewfinder. A good recommendation for beginners is, if an LCD is available, use it to align your image before taking a picture. With a majority of digital cameras, the LCD does represent the actual captured image.

If you find you prefer to use a viewfinder, most digital cameras with an LCD screen will also have a viewfinder available. Also, there are some situations where using the viewfinder may be appropriate.

Reasons to Use the Viewfinder
1. In some circumstances, the LCD simply may not be an option. If it is too sunny and it's impossible to see the LCD because the LCD is not bright enough, the digital camera user may have to rely on the viewfinder to align the picture.
2. On the other hand, it may be too dark to take a picture. In this case, the person taking the picture may be relying on the flash, and cannot view

the persons or objects that he/she wishes to capture in the picture. The viewfinder may be a more accurate way to make sure everyone/everything is included in the shot.

3. Finally, you can use the viewfinder when the LCD is turned off during picture taking (a good option for battery conservation). When the LCD is off, the image must be captured using the viewfinder. Typically, once the picture is taken, the LCD will display the image for a period of 5-10 seconds so you can check to make certain that the image you intended to capture was actually captured.

Taking a picture with the LCD off is an opportunity for a digital camera user to gauge how well the LCD and viewfinder are calibrated (or not calibrated). Simply stated, if pictures thought to be captured through the viewfinder appear the same on the LCD, then the LCD and viewfinder are in sync. If every picture taken using the viewfinder appears off center on the LCD, the LCD and viewfinder are out of sync.

Remember, for the majority of digital cameras, the LCD represents what will actually appear when the pictures are transferred to a computer. This is why you should use the LCD if it is available.

Chapter 9

Digital Camera Functions and Menus

What You Will Learn in This Chapter:
- ✓ Reviewing pictures immediately
- ✓ Deleting pictures immediately
- ✓ Using Playback mode

Section 18: Instantly Review Pictures on Your Digital Camera

Once a picture is taken, the LCD immediately displays the captured image. You will typically have 5-10 seconds to view the picture just taken. After 5-10 seconds, the picture is automatically stored.

NOTE: *After taking a picture, the image will be shown on the LCD* <u>*regardless*</u> *of whether the LCD was on when the picture was taken.*

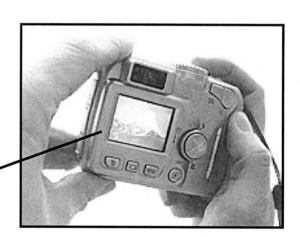

Pictures are displayed on the LCD automatically for up to 10 seconds after being taken.

Immediately after snapping a picture, you may delete the image if you don't like it. This can be done in the 5-10 seconds when the image is displayed on the LCD. This feature is one of the biggest benefits of using a digital camera instead of a traditional film camera.

The picture may not be centered, the lighting may be off, the people in the picture may blink or forget to smile, your finger got in the way, etc. Whatever the reason, if you do not like the picture, just delete it! This "immediate delete" feature opens up space on the digital camera's memory for pictures that you do want to keep.

In addition to deleting pictures within the 5-10 second time frame, you have the opportunity to delete pictures later from the LCD (in playback mode) or later still after the pictures are transferred to your computer.

Reviewing Pictures Instantly: Step-by-Step Instructions
1. **Take a picture with the digital camera.**
2. **Look at the LCD to review the picture immediately after taking.**
3. **The digital camera will automatically revert to picture taking mode after 5-10 seconds if no action is taken to delete the picture.**

Section 19: Deleting a Picture from your Digital Camera

Some pictures just don't turn out right. Good news! You can simply delete them from your digital camera right after they are taken.

It is important to delete the pictures you are not interested in keeping. The main reason to delete unwanted pictures is to open up space in your digital camera memory for other pictures. However, it will also save you time when you transfer pictures to your computer because you won't be transferring pictures that you don't want anyway. Follow the step-by-step guide to delete a picture from your digital camera.

Deleting a Picture Immediately: Step-by-Step Instructions

1. Take the picture.
2. Look at the LCD to review the picture.
3. Press the ENTER or OK button on the digital camera when the picture is being viewed.
4. Use the Up and Down Arrow buttons to navigate to the delete image icon (trash can).
5. Press ENTER or OK to delete the picture from the digital camera.
   a. Some digital cameras require a last step by asking you if you are sure that you want to delete the image.
   b. Other digital cameras will make you confirm that you only want to delete the single image and not all of the images in memory.

Deleting a Picture Immediately: Visual Guide

Step One:
Take the
picture.

Step Two:
Look at the
LCD to review
the picture.

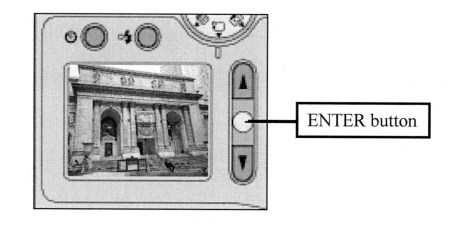

ENTER button

Step Three:
Press the
ENTER or OK
button on the
camera.

Step Four:
Use the Up and Down Arrow buttons to navigate to the delete image icon. (This icon may be pictured as a trash can.)

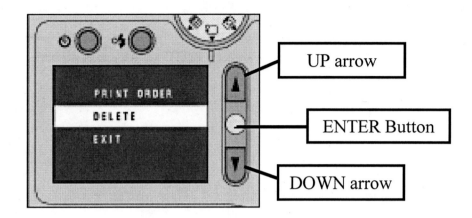

Step Five:
Use the Up and Down arrows to move to **CURRENT PICTURE.** Press the middle 'OK' or 'ENTER' button to delete the current picture only.

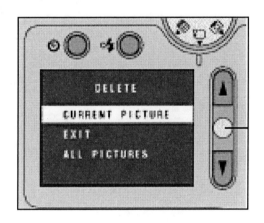

Reviewing Pictures in Playback Mode

After taking some pictures, you can review them in playback mode. Playback mode allows you to scroll through all of the images you have taken and select which pictures you would like to delete.

In playback mode, users can not only delete pictures, but can also magnify pictures. After activating the playback mode, you can scroll through pictures by using the digital camera's arrow buttons.

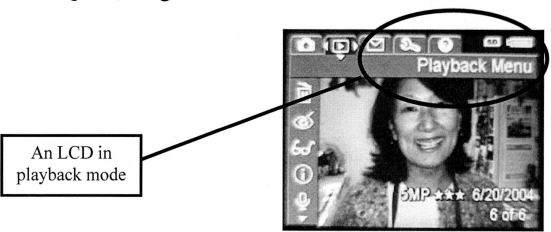

An LCD in playback mode

Reviewing Pictures in Playback Mode: Step-by-Step Instructions

1. Make sure the digital camera is powered on.
2. Press the "Review" or "OK" button.
3. The first picture taken will appear on the LCD.
4. Scroll through the pictures using the directional or arrow buttons.

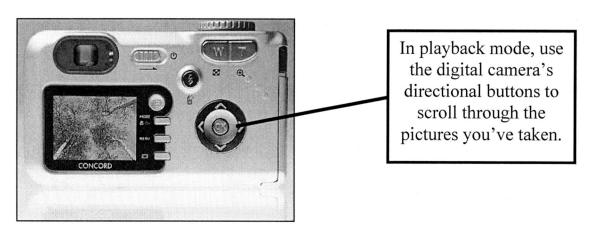

In playback mode, use the digital camera's directional buttons to scroll through the pictures you've taken.

Deleting a Picture in Playback Mode

Once you have learned to scroll through all your pictures in playback mode, you'll recognize that the process of deleting a picture in playback mode is identical to the process of deleting a picture directly after it has been taken.

Deleting a Picture in Playback Mode: Step-by-Step Instructions

1. Press the "Review" or "OK" button.
2. The first picture taken will appear on the LCD.
3. Scroll through the pictures using the directional or arrow buttons.

4. When the picture you choose to delete is displayed, press **ENTER** or **OK** to delete the picture from the digital camera.

    a. Some digital cameras require a last step by asking you if you are sure that you want to delete the image.

    b. Other digital cameras will make you confirm that you only want to delete the single image and not all of the images in memory.

Deleting a Picture in Playback Mode: Visual Guide

Step One:
Press the OK button.

Step Two:
Scroll through the pictures using the directional or arrow buttons

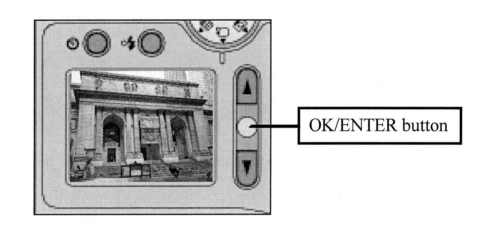

OK/ENTER button

Step Three:
Press the ENTER or OK button on the camera.

Step Four:
Use the Up and Down Arrow buttons to navigate to the delete image icon. (This icon may be pictured as a trash can.)

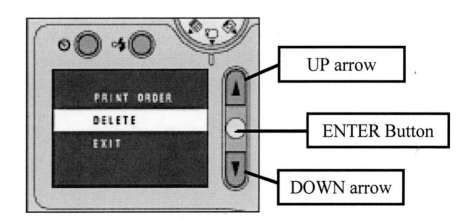

UP arrow

ENTER Button

DOWN arrow

Step Five:
Use the Up and Down arrows to move to CURRENT PICTURE.
Press the middle 'OK' or 'ENTER' button to delete the current picture only.

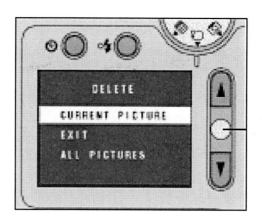

Section 20: Overview of Digital Camera Menus

In general, digital cameras use a series of similar menus and icons to guide you through picture taking. While these menu options and icons may differ slightly from digital camera to digital camera, they all operate on the same basic principles.

- Use directional or arrow buttons to scroll through your menus.
- Highlight an item to select it.
- Press the OK button to perform an action.

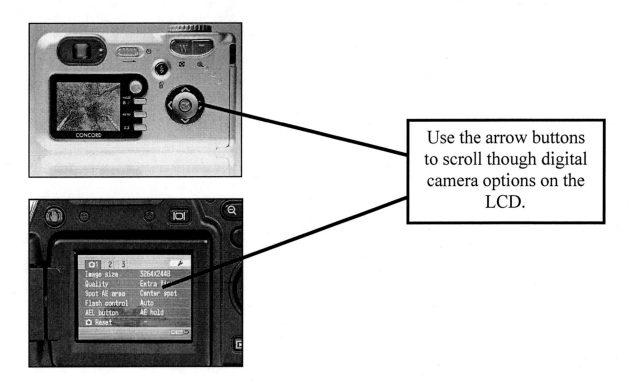

Use the arrow buttons to scroll though digital camera options on the LCD.

Manual Buttons

Some digital cameras may have manual buttons, found on the outside of the camera, for features such as *flash*, *picture timer*, and *delete* instead of listing these options on the LCD.

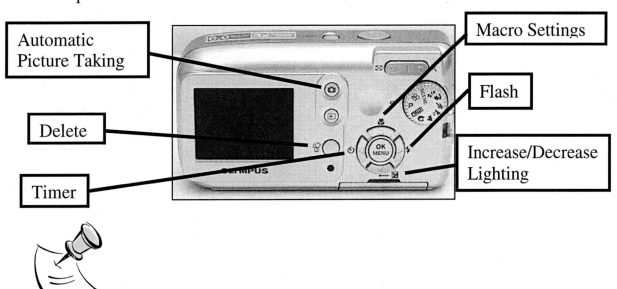

Automatic Picture Taking

Macro Settings

Flash

Delete

Increase/Decrease Lighting

Timer

NOTE: The digital camera shown here uses several manual buttons for the camera options. Manual options are those not listed on the LCD.

Chapter 9: Digital Camera Functions and Menus

The digital camera pictured on the previous page has manual buttons for Automatic Picture Taking (camera icon), Flash (lightning bolt icon), Timer (timer icon), Macro Settings (flower icon), Increasing/Decreasing Lighting (+ and – icon), and Delete (trash can icon).

When manual buttons are available, simply use these buttons as if they were menu items. Buttons may actually simplify the use of some digital cameras.

Chapter 10

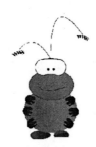

Using External Memory

What You Will Learn in This Chapter:
- ✓ Installing external memory
- ✓ Transferring pictures to external memory
- ✓ Taking pictures with external memory
- ✓ Transferring pictures from external memory to the computer

Section 21: Using an External Memory Card

Previous sections discussed external memory, measuring external memory, and the benefits to using external memory. This section, will take you through a step-by-step guide to using external memory.

Inserting a Memory Card

The process of inserting a memory card is very similar to loading a new roll of film. The one difference is that you need to make sure the digital camera is powered off before you begin.

Inserting a Memory Card: Step-by-Step Instructions

1. **Turn your digital camera OFF.**
2. **Open your memory card door located on the camera. This door is usually located near the batteries.**
3. **Insert the memory card into the digital camera.**
4. **Close the memory card door.**
5. **Turn on the digital camera.**

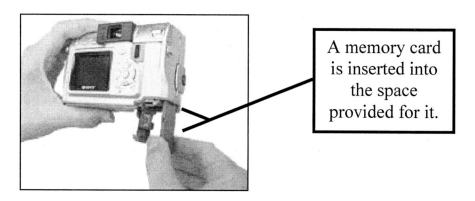

A memory card is inserted into the space provided for it.

Transferring Pictures to a Memory Card

If you have images stored on your internal memory and you insert an external memory card, the digital camera will prompt you to transfer the images stored on your camera to your external memory card.

Once you transfer images from internal memory to an external memory card, the images are deleted from your digital camera's internal memory, opening space for new pictures.

Removing a Memory Card: Step-by-Step Instructions
1. **Make sure the digital camera is off.**
2. **Open the memory card door located on the digital camera, usually near the batteries.**
3. **Push the EJECT button next to the external memory card. (Some cameras do not have an eject button, for those, just push the card in a little bit and the card will eject itself.)**
4. **Take out the card and close the door.**

Taking Pictures with the Memory Card Inserted
The picture taking process does not change after you insert the external memory card. Simply take pictures as you would normally.

A digital camera will automatically store all pictures taken on your external memory card once it has been inserted. This also means that pictures will no longer be stored on the digital camera's internal memory.

NOTE: The next section takes a quick look at transferring pictures from a memory card. This is being done to improve your general understanding of digital cameras. Chapter 13 will review transferring pictures in greater detail.

Methods to Transfer Pictures from a Memory Card to a Computer
Once pictures have been taken, the pictures stored on external memory cards can be transferred or unloaded to a computer using a number of different methods. The method you should choose to use will depend on the options available with your camera and your general comfort level with the process.

First, you can transfer pictures while leaving the memory card in the digital camera. Instead of removing the card, you use a cable (or camera dock) to transfer pictures directly from the digital camera to the computer. The pictures on the external memory card will automatically be transferred to the computer.

One end of a cable is inserted into the camera, while the other end is inserted into the computer.

A second method to transfer pictures is to take the memory card out of the camera. Once the card has been removed, you can put it directly into a drive or "slot" in the computer tower.

A third way to transfer pictures is to use a card reader. A card reader is a separate piece of equipment that is made for transferring pictures. One end of a card reader is plugged into the computer. The other end is a slot specially designed for a memory card. Remove the external memory card from the digital camera and insert the card directly into the base of card reader. The pictures will be transferred.

Finally, you do not have to transfer the pictures to your computer at all. Some memory cards can be inserted directly into a printer to print photos. This relationship between memory card and printer is typical when the two devices have the same manufacturer.

Chapter 10: Using External Memory

Chapter 11

Digital Camera Software

What You Will Learn in This Chapter:
- ✓ Hardware vs. Software
- ✓ Digital camera software
- ✓ Digital camera software vs. photo editing software
- ✓ Installing software

Section 22: Digital Camera Hardware vs. Software

What is Hardware?

Hardware includes all the physical parts of a digital camera. The memory, the LCD, the knobs, the viewfinder, and the carrying strap are all parts of the hardware. Every piece of the digital camera you can touch and feel is classified as hardware.

When referring to a computer, hardware includes the monitor, keyboard, mouse, cables, and tower.

What is Software?

When you purchase a digital camera, you also receive software (also called programs) stored on a compact disk (CD). The software files on the CD are specific electronic instructions for your computer. You are unable to physically see these files, although they are imprinted on the CD.

NOTE: Electronic instructions for your computer are referred to as software, software packages, or programs. In stores or online, software is purchased in book-sized boxes, which usually contain a CD. The CD contains the software.

When software is *installed,* or copied into a computer, it gives the computer user specific capabilities which vary depending on the type of software installed.

Types of Software Needed for Your Digital Camera

There are two separate programs (software) needed in order to use your digital camera with your computer. These two programs are *digital camera* software and *photo editing* software. Each piece of software provides specific abilities. Digital camera software allows you to transfer pictures from your digital camera to your computer. Editing software allows you to edit, or make changes, to your pictures.

They may come together on one compact disc or be separated into two compact discs.

Digital Camera Software   **Photo Editing Software**

Section 23: Installing Software

Installing software is relatively simple. Insert the CD into the CD drive (or port) on your computer and follow the instructions that appear on your computer screen.

Chapter 11: Digital Camera Software

Important Points to Remember When Installing ANY Software

- Close all windows and programs before inserting the CD into your computer.
- Read, read, and read!!! The computer will walk you through the entire process. Follow the directions.
- 95% of the time all you have to do is click the NEXT button or the OK button.

Important Points Relating to Digital Camera Software

- The digital camera must be able to interact (be able to send and receive messages) with your computer.
- Digital camera software must be installed onto your computer to enable your digital camera and computer to interact.
- All digital cameras come with this software.
- The digital camera software comes on a CD, or compact disc, which will be in the box that came with the digital camera.

Every person reading *Basic Digital Cameras for Beginners* may own a unique digital camera model. Although we would like to provide step-by-step directions for each digital camera, there are simply too many variations. However, digital camera software is typically very user-friendly and walks you through the steps to complete the installation.

Installing Digital Camera Software: Step-by-Step Instructions

1. **Place the CD into your computer's CD Drive. The software will begin loading. A bar will move across the screen indicating the software's progress.**
2. **The computer will walk you through all of the steps needed to install the software. Follow along, answer any questions, and click the NEXT or OK buttons.**
3. **The computer will indicate when the installation is complete.**
4. **An icon of the digital camera software will appear on your desktop. Remove the CD when the installation is complete.**

NOTE: Unless the software requires the digital camera be connected during installation, do not connect the camera to the computer. You will connect the camera after you have installed the photo editing software.

Installing Digital Camera Software: Visual Guide

Step One: Place the CD into your computer's CD Drive.

The software will begin loading. A bar will move across the screen indicating its progress.

Step Two: The computer will walk you through the steps needed to install the software.

Generally, follow along, answer any questions, and click the NEXT or OK buttons.

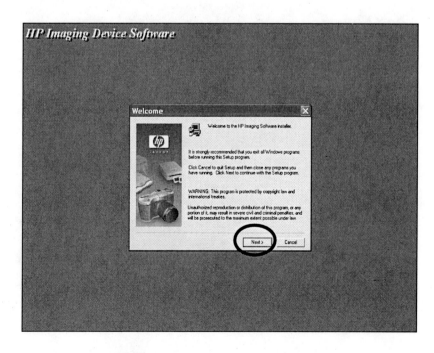

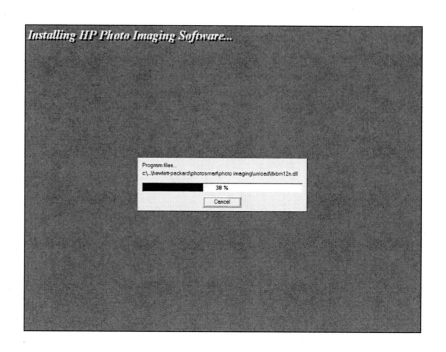

Step Three:
The computer
will indicate
when the
installation is
complete.

Step Four:
An icon of the
digital camera
software will
appear on your
desktop.

Remove the
CD when the
installation is
complete.

Section 24: Photo Editing Software

All digital cameras come with software that allows you to add effects, edit, and save your pictures.

Important Points Related to Photo Editing Software
- Photo editing software always comes with a new digital camera.
- The software comes on a CD, compact disc, in the box that came with the digital camera.
- It enables you to alter your images: get rid of red-eye, change image brightness, contrast, color, backgrounds, etc.
- Examples of photo editing software:
    a. Adobe Photodeluxe, Adobe Photoshop
    b. Photo Express
    c. Microsoft Picture It!
    d. Picassa (free version available at www.Google.com)

Where Can You Acquire Photo Editing Software?
1. On a CD sold in stores.
2. On a CD with the purchase of a digital camera.
3. For download over the Internet. Some downloadable versions are free.

Chapter 11: Digital Camera Software

Chapter 12

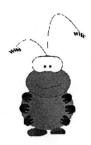

Picassa

What You Will Learn in This Chapter:
✓ What is Picassa?
✓ Steps to download Picassa
✓ Steps to install Picassa

Section 25: Picassa Software

For standardization, this book will use "Picassa." Picassa is free digital imaging software available on the Internet at www.Google.com.

As you'll soon learn, Picassa makes picture editing easy. It is a great program to use to edit and manipulate pictures. Picassa is recommended for basic photo editing by beginners and intermediate users. Even if you already have a photo editing program with your digital camera, you may want to follow these steps to download and use Picassa. You can then compare Picassa to your own photo editing program and choose to use the one which best meets your needs.

NOTE: As mentioned, Picassa is great for editing pictures. To organize, delete, and rename pictures, most people use their My Pictures folder. A section on using the My Pictures Folder is included later in this book.

Downloading Picassa: Step-by-Step Instructions
1. **Using the Start menu, click on Internet Explorer.**
2. **Type www.Google.com in the address bar and then press the Enter key on the keyboard.**
3. **Click the MORE link above the search field.**
4. **In the list, find and click on the PICASSA link.**

5. Click FREE DOWNLOAD.
6. Click on the CLICK HERE TO GET IT GOING link.
7. Click the SAVE button.
8. In the Save in: box, select DESKTOP from drop-down list.
9. Click the SAVE button.

Downloading Picassa: Visual Guide

**Step One:
Using the Start
menu, click on
INTERNET
EXPLORER.**

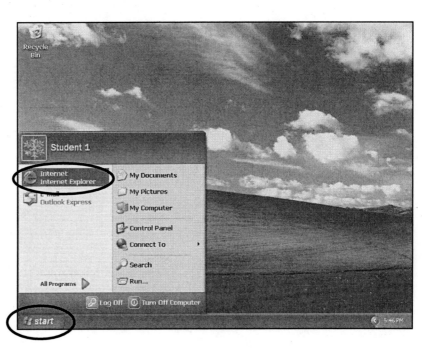

**Step Two:
Type
www.Google.com
in the address bar
and then press the
ENTER key on
the keyboard.**

Chapter 12: Picassa

**Step Three:
Click on the
MORE link
above the
search field.**

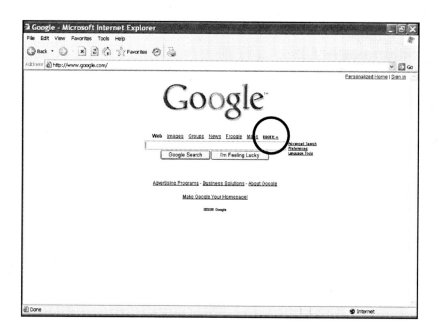

**Step Four:
Find and
click on the
PICASSA
link.**

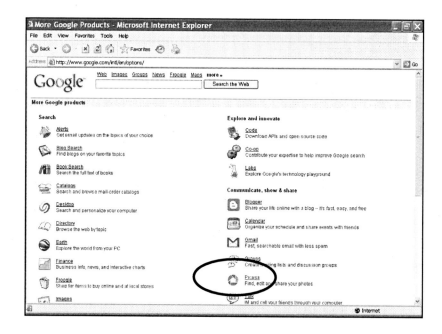

**Step Five:
Click the
FREE
DOWNLOAD
link.**

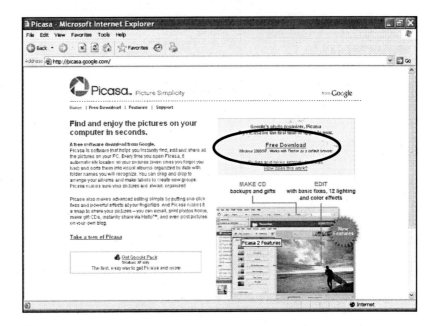

**Step Six:
Click the
CLICK
HERE TO
GET IT
GOING link.**

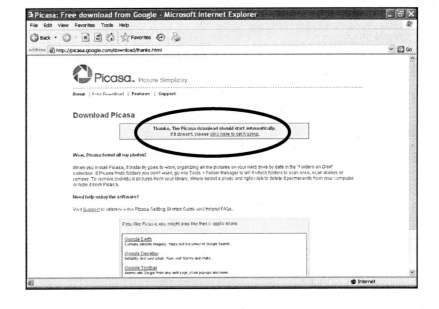

**Step Seven:
Click the
SAVE button.**

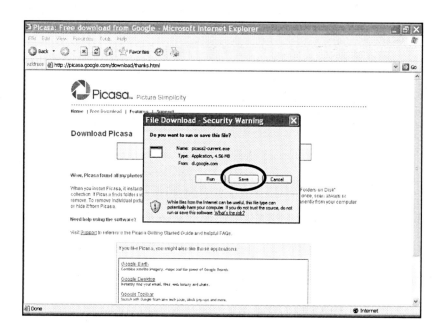

**Step Eight:
In the Save in:
box, select
DESKTOP from
drop-down list.**

**Step Nine:
Click the SAVE
button.**

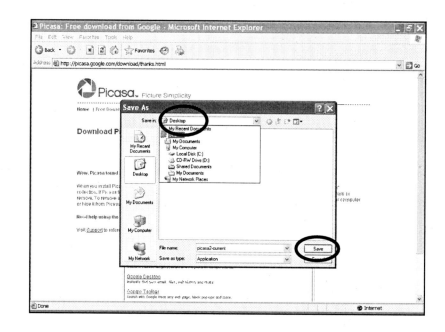

A bar will move across your screen. When it is done, you have finished downloading Picassa. Congratulations! Now, you will need to install the program.

Chapter 12: Picassa

Installing Picassa

To get Picassa to work on your computer, you need to install the program. Installing a program is the process of placing the program files where they belong on the computer's hard drive. This will allow you to access and use the program when needed.

Installing Picassa: Step-by-Step Guide

1. Find the Picassa icon on the desktop by closing all open windows.
2. Double-click on the Picassa icon to begin.
3. Click the RUN button.
4. Click the I AGREE button on the license agreement.
5. Click on the INSTALL button. The software will be installed, as indicated by the status bar.
6. Uncheck each box, except the RUN PICASSA box (Optional Step).
7. Click on the FINISH button to complete installation.
8. Make sure the dot is in front of the "Completely scan my computer for pictures" option. When Picassa opens, click on the CONTINUE button.

Installing Picassa: Visual Guide

Step One:
Find the Picassa icon on the desktop by closing any open windows.

Step Two:
Double-click on the Picassa icon to begin installation.

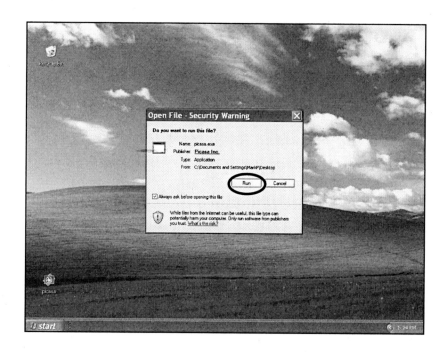

**Step Three:
Click the
RUN
button.**

**Step Four:
Click the I
AGREE
button.**

**Step Five:
Click the
INSTALL
button.**

**The software
will be
installed, as
indicated by
the status
bar.**

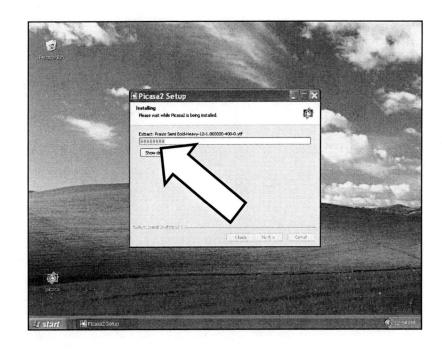

Optional Installation Recommendation: *Uncheck all boxes except the box titled "Run Picassa." Unchecking is done by clicking once on each checkmark in the small boxes next to each command. The checkmarks will disappear.*

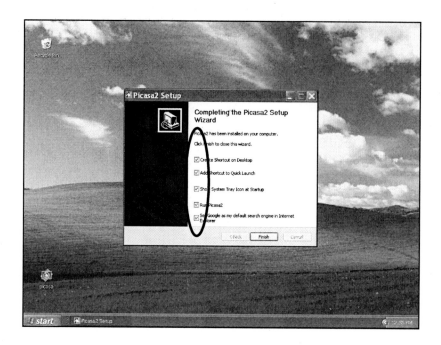

Optional Step Six:
Uncheck each box, except the RUN PICASSA box.

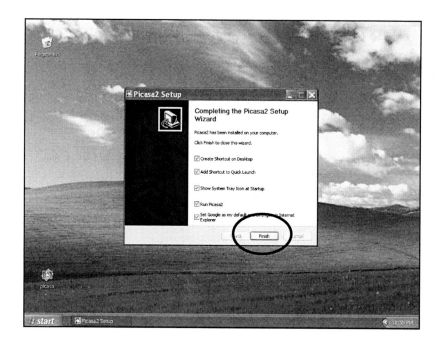

Step Seven:
Click on the FINISH button to complete installation.

Step Eight:
Make sure the dot is in front of the "Completely scan my computer for pictures" option.

Click the CONTINUE button.

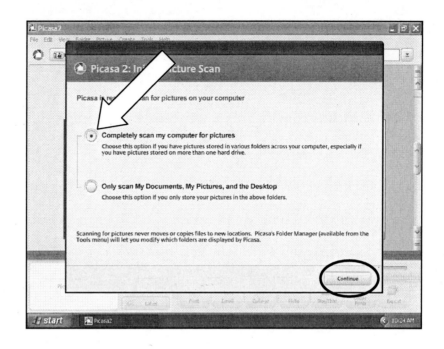

Picassa will automatically open and perform a search for any pictures already stored on your computer. This includes pictures you have saved, clip art, and any sample pictures that were on the computer when you purchased it.

Once Picassa has found the stored images, a copy of each picture will be stored in Picassa automatically. This is known as your Picassa *picture library*.

NOTE: If Picassa does not automatically open, you may use the Start Menu to access the program, as identified in the next chapter.

Congratulations, you now have a new photo editing program!

Chapter 12: Picassa

Chapter 13

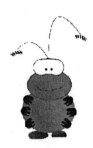

Accessing Picassa and Transferring Pictures from Your Digital Camera

What You Will Learn in This Chapter:
✓ Opening Picassa
✓ Transferring pictures from your digital camera, using Picassa
✓ Importing pictures stored on your computer to Picassa

Section 26: Accessing Picassa

Start Menu

You can access any installed digital camera software from your START menu. Your software will be listed in the PROGRAMS menu.

Opening Picassa: Step-by-Step Instructions

1. Click the START button.
2. Move to ALL PROGRAMS.
3. In the submenu to the right, slide the arrow onto the PICASSA option.
4. Slide your mouse pointer into the new submenu that appears to the right. Place it over the option PICASSA. Click once with your left mouse button.
   a. If you have never opened Picassa before, Picassa will open and search for any pictures on your computer.
   b. If you have opened Picassa before, Picassa will open to your most recent folder.

Opening Picassa: Visual Guide

Chapter 13: Accessing Picassa and Transferring Pictures from Your Digital Camera

Step One:
Click the
START button.

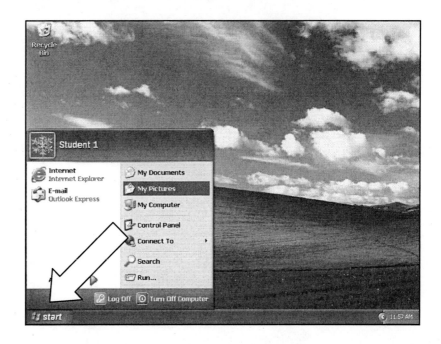

Step Two:
Slide the mouse
arrow to ALL
PROGRAMS.

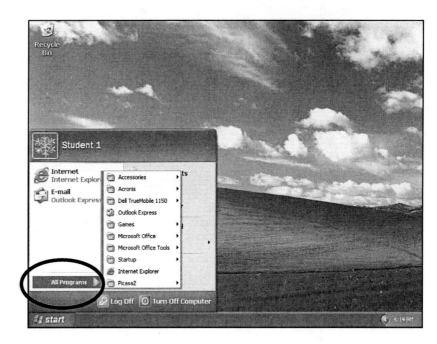

Step Three:
Slide the arrow onto the PICASSA option.

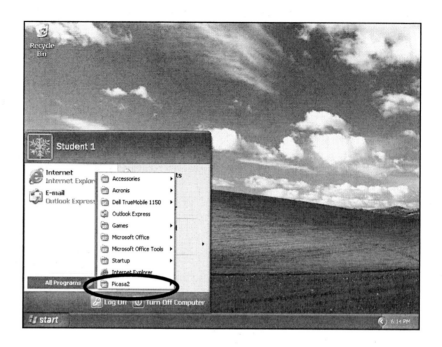

Step Four:
Slide your mouse pointer into the new submenu that appears to the right.

Place it over the option PICASSA.

Click once with your left mouse

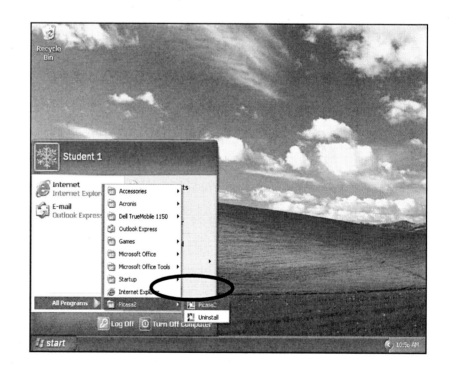

**Step 4A:
Picassa will
open and
automatically
search for
pictures on
your computer,
as shown on
the search bar.**

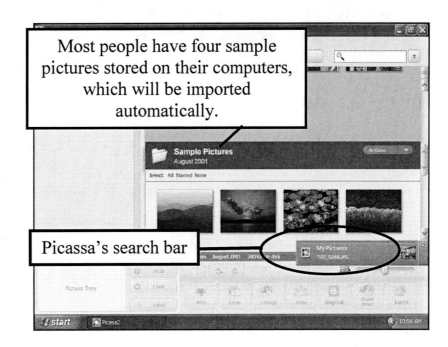

Most people have four sample pictures stored on their computers, which will be imported automatically.

Picassa's search bar

NOTE: Picassa will show a search bar indicating that it is searching and importing all pictures located on your computer.
The first time, and every time thereafter, the Picassa program is opened, the program will perform a search of your computer for any picture files.

These files may be located in the My Pictures folder or elsewhere on the computer's hard drive. Most computers have a Sample folder of pictures that will be automatically imported into Picassa for editing.

Picassa will find all picture files on your computer and automatically import them, even though many of them may not be edited. This is a terrific feature for a beginner because you don't have to search your computer manually for pictures to edit them.

Section 27: Moving Pictures from Your Digital Camera to Your Computer

Once you have taken pictures and installed all the software on your computer, you must move the pictures from your digital camera to your computer for editing. The ability to edit pictures is a fantastic benefit of using a digital camera.

To edit pictures you have taken with your digital camera, you must transfer the pictures from your digital camera to your computer.

All digital camera software will include a program to aid in the transfer of pictures. This book uses the Picassa program to transfer pictures from your digital camera to your computer. No matter what program your digital camera has, the transfer steps will be very similar to Picassa.

If you have followed the steps and installed both Picassa and your digital camera software, you will be able to import pictures using Picassa.

Chapter 13: Accessing Picassa and Transferring Pictures from Your Digital Camera

Transferring Pictures to Your Computer

To transfer pictures from your digital camera to your computer, first make sure the digital camera is powered off, and then follow the steps listed below.

Transferring Pictures from Your Digital Camera to Your Computer: Step-by-Step Instructions

1. Make sure your digital cameral is powered off.
2. Attach the skinny end of the USB transfer cable to the digital camera. Attach the opposite end of the USB cable to the USB port on the computer.
3. Open Picassa using the Start Menu.
   a. Select START.
   b. Move to ALL PROGRAMS.
   c. Slide the arrow to the list of programs.
   d. Click once on PICASSA to select the program.
4. Turn on the digital camera.
   a. If a pop-up window appears, close the window by clicking on the "X" in the upper right corner of the window. This may be your digital camera software automatically opening to aid in the transfer of pictures to your computer. As mentioned, you will use the Picassa program to import pictures instead.
5. Click on the IMPORT button at the top left portion of the window.
6. Click on SELECT DEVICE on the top left portion of the new window.
7. Select your digital camera from the list by clicking on the appropriate digital camera name. The pictures on the digital camera will show up in the picture tray.
8. Click on the FINISH button on the lower left-hand portion of the window.
9. Type a folder title for the pictures you are importing, e.g. "Camping Trip," "Beach Pictures," or "Halloween."
10. Click the FINISH button in the dialogue box.
11. Turn off the digital camera and unplug it from the computer.

Your pictures are now in the Picassa program on your computer. You may now continue to edit, change, and save your pictures.

NOTE: A copy of all transferred pictures will also appear in the MY PICTURES folder, accessible through the START menu and described in the chapter on using the My Pictures folder. These are unedited, original copies. Any changes you make to the pictures in Picassa will not be transferred to these originals.

Transferring Pictures from Your Digital Camera to Your Computer: Visual Guide

Step One:
Turn the digital camera off.

Step Two:
Connect your digital camera to the computer using the USB cable.

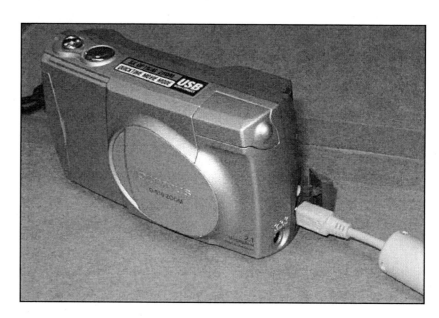

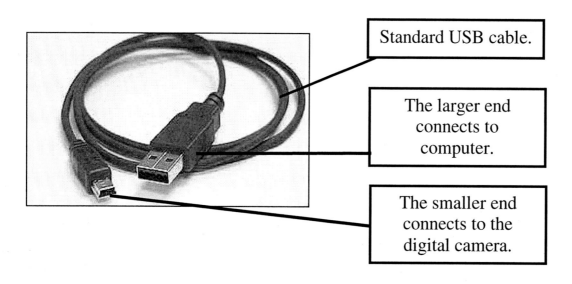

Standard USB cable.

The larger end connects to computer.

The smaller end connects to the digital camera.

Chapter 13: Accessing Picassa and Transferring Pictures from Your Digital Camera

Step Three: Open Picassa using the START menu.

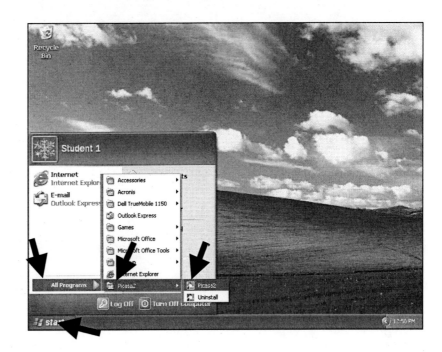

Step Four: Turn the digital camera on. Close any pop-up windows that may open automatically.

Step Five: After opening Picassa, click the IMPORT button.

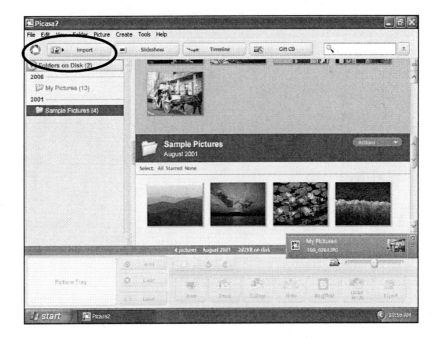

Step Six: Click the **SELECT DEVICE** button.

Step Seven: Find the name your of digital camera in the drop-down menu. Click on it.

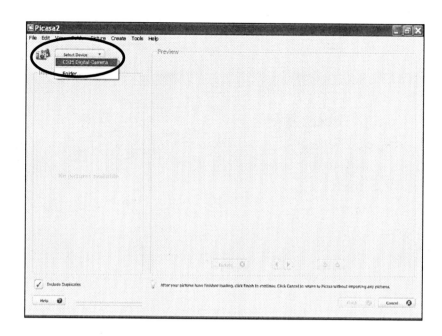

Once the device (camera) is selected, pictures will be transferred from the digital camera.

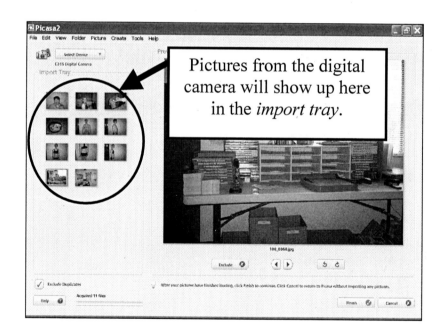

Pictures from the digital camera will show up here in the *import tray*.

**Step Eight:
Click on
FINISH**

All pictures in the import tray will be transferred from the digital camera to your computer.

**Step Nine:
The transferred
pictures will
appear in a
folder in Picassa.
Type the name
you want to give
the folder.**
(*e.g.* **"Camping
Trip," "Beach
Pictures," or
"Halloween."**)

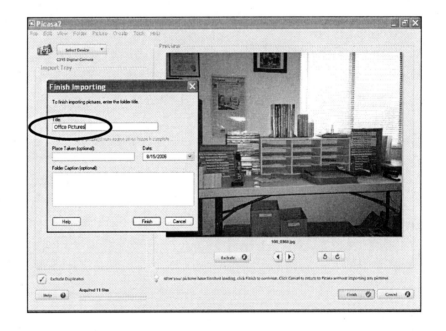

Step Ten: Click on FINISH in the dialogue box.

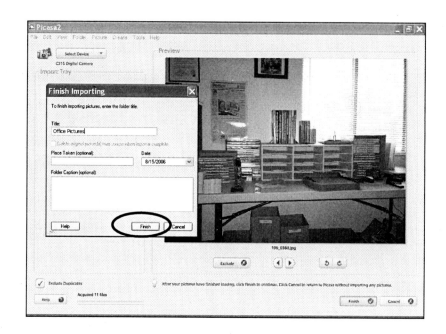

Step Eleven: Turn off the digital camera to save your batteries.

Your pictures will be imported from your digital camera to Picassa.

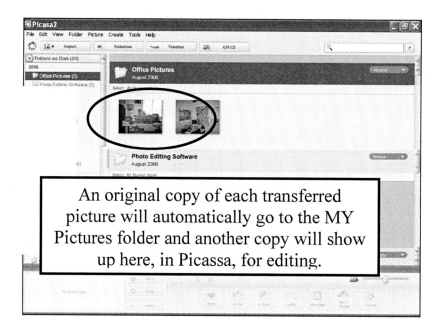

An original copy of each transferred picture will automatically go to the MY Pictures folder and another copy will show up here, in Picassa, for editing.

NOTE: Picassa does not give you the ability to delete pictures from your digital camera once you have imported them. You must delete the pictures from the digital camera manually after you have transferred them.

Your pictures are now on the computer. Super job!

Chapter 14

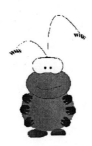

Photo Editing

What You Will Learn in This Chapter:
- ✓ Becoming comfortable with Picassa
- ✓ Browsing through pictures
- ✓ Opening pictures
- ✓ Performing basic photo editing tasks

Section 28: Photo Editing in Picassa

Editing Pictures

You have quickly reached the Editing stage of the four-stage picture saving process. In this stage, you will learn how to edit the pictures you have already taken and transferred.

Editing gives you the opportunity to manipulate pictures to enhance their quality. This chapter reviews the common tasks performed in photo editing.

All of these editing tasks are available in Picassa, as well as all other photo editing programs. So, the information you gather and skills you acquire here will be beneficial no matter which program you use for photo editing.

Browsing Through Images Using Picassa

Once you have your photo editing software opened, you can view your photos as a group or individually. Most photo editing programs enable you to view individual pictures by double clicking them. This is true with the Picassa program.

Opening Pictures for Editing Using Picassa: Step-by-Step Instructions

1. **Open Picassa.**
2. **Click on the folder that you wish to browse through at the left side of the window.**
3. **Double click on the picture you wish to view.**
   - **The picture will appear enlarged in the main portion of the window.**

Opening Pictures for Editing Using Picassa: Visual Guide

Step One:
Open Picassa,
if not already
open.

Step Two:
Click on the
folder you wish
to browse
through, such
as "My
Pictures" or
"Sample
Pictures."

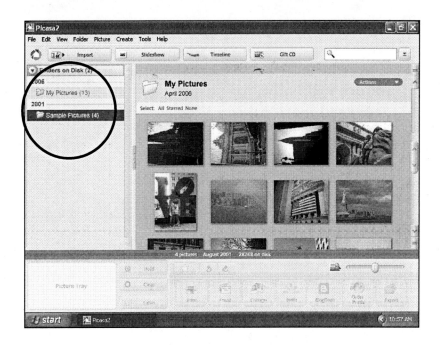

Step Three:
The pictures
will appear to
the right of the
folder bar.

Double click on
the picture you
wish to
view/edit.

The selected picture will be enlarged for editing purposes.

Browsing Though Pictures

In most instances, you will want to return to the picture library after editing or viewing a single picture. In this section, you will learn how to browse through your pictures in Picassa.

You may choose to browse through images in a slideshow like fashion, or return to the picture library to select from a layout of pictures.

Returning to the Picture Library after Viewing/Editing Pictures: Step-by-Step Instructions

1. Double click the picture you intend to view or edit.
2. After viewing or editing, return to the pictures by double clicking on BACK TO LIBRARY button.

Returning to the Picture Library after Viewing/Editing Pictures: Visual Guide

Step One:
Double click the picture you want to view or edit.

Step Two:
After viewing or editing the picture, click the BACK TO LIBRARY button.

You will be
able to browse
through all the
pictures.

Browsing Through Pictures Using Arrow Buttons

You may also browse though pictures in Picassa using the arrow buttons at the
top of the screen. Using the arrows allows you to browse in more of a
"slideshow" fashion. The right arrow will open the next picture in the library
and the left arrow will open the previous picture in the library.

Browsing Through Pictures Using Arrow Buttons: Step-by-Step Instructions

1. Double click a picture to view or edit.
2. After viewing or editing the picture, click on the right arrow
   button to open the next picture in the library.
3. After viewing or editing the picture, click on the right arrow to
   continue through the library.
4. Use the left arrow to reverse your navigation through the
   library.

Browsing Through Images Using Arrow Buttons: Visual Guide

Step One: Double click a picture to view or edit.

Step Two: After viewing or editing the picture, click on the right arrow button to open the next picture in the library.

Step Three: After viewing or editing the picture, click on the right arrow to continue through the library.

Step Four: Use the left arrow to reverse your navigation through the library.

Section 29: Basic Photo Editing Features

Now that you have taken pictures, transferred them to your computer, and know how to select them, you are ready to do some basic photo editing in the Picassa program.

Rotating Pictures

You can rotate your pictures 90, 180, 270, or 360 degrees. Rotating a picture is helpful when a digital camera picture was taken sideways.

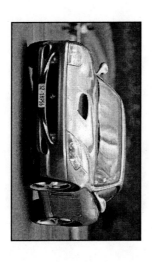   Vs.

Rotating Pictures in Picassa: Step-by-Step Instructions

1. Select the picture you wish to rotate by double-clicking on it.
2. Click the curved arrow button once to rotate the picture 90 degrees. If needed, click again to rotate another 90 degrees.
3. Go back to the picture library by clicking BACK TO LIBRARY.

Rotating Pictures in Picassa: Visual Guide

Step One:
Double click
on the picture
you want to
rotate.

Step Two:
Once the picture
is open, click one
of the rotate
buttons in the
lower portion of
the window.

The picture will be rotated. Stop when the picture is in the upright or desired position.

Step Three: Click on the BACK TO LIBRARY button.

The picture will be saved in the rotated position.

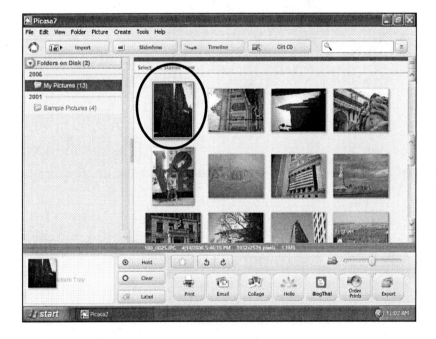

Cropping

Cropping is useful to get rid of, or cut away, extra space in a picture. Cropping is also useful in straightening pictures that may have been taken off-center.

Cropping definition: To cut out a portion of a picture.
- Widely used to eliminate "extra" space in a picture.
- Bill Gates photo example below. If you only want the picture of a young Bill Gates, but not the rest of his family, you can crop them out of the picture.

Vs.

Be cautious when cropping a picture. It is important to recognize that when you crop a picture, you may also lower the quality of the final picture.

This typically happens when you crop a small area from a large photograph, as shown below. This is similar to looking through a magnifying glass at a printed picture or zooming far into a picture.

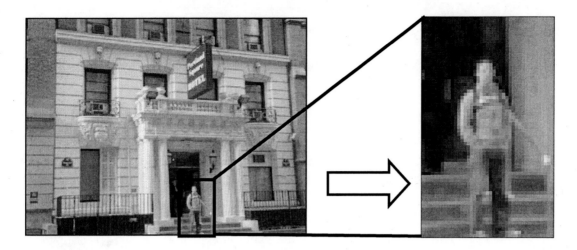

NOTE: Cropping too much of a picture can result in a much lower quality remnant, as illustrated in the picture above.

Cropping a Picture in Picassa: Step-by-Step Instructions
1. Double click the image to open the picture.
2. Click the CROP button.
3. Place you mouse pointer in the upper left corner of the portion of the picture you want cropped. Click and drag your mouse arrow to the opposite (bottom right) corner of the picture.
4. An outlined box will appear as you drag.
5. Let go of the left mouse button when you have the area you want cropped outlined.
6. Click the APPLY button to finish cropping the picture.

Chapter 14: Photo Editing

Cropping a Picture in Picassa: Visual Guide

Step One:
Select the picture you want to crop by double clicking on it.

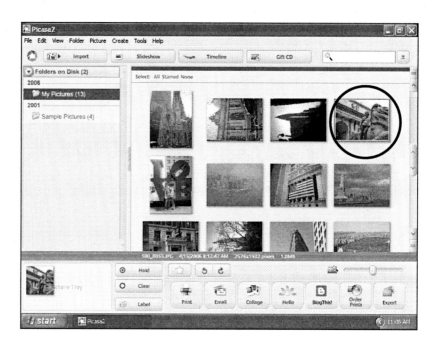

Step Two:
Click the CROP button.

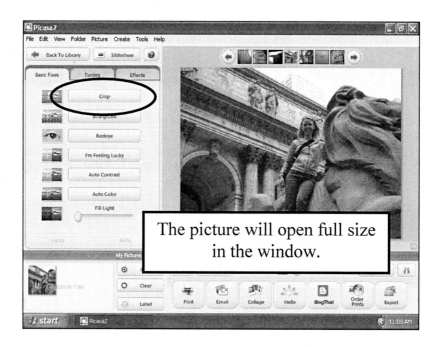

The picture will open full size in the window.

**Step Three:
Select the
upper left-most
point of the
area you want
cropped.**

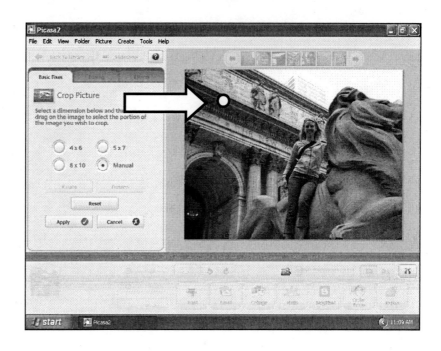

**Step Four:
Click and drag
at a 45 degree
angle down
and to the
right.**

**The image will
be clearer in
the portion of
the picture that
you are
selecting.**

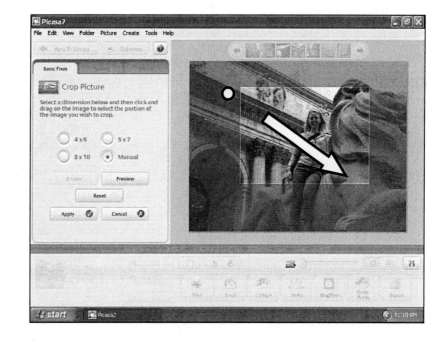

Step Five:
Release the
mouse button
when you have
reached the
bottom right-
most portion of
the cropped
area.

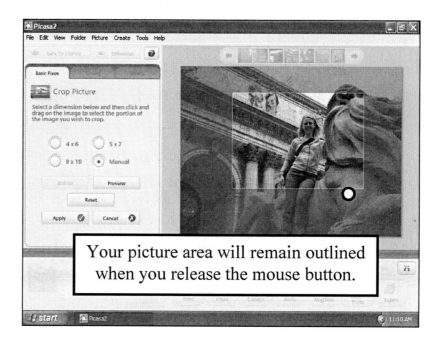

Your picture area will remain outlined
when you release the mouse button.

Step Six:
Click on the
APPLY button.

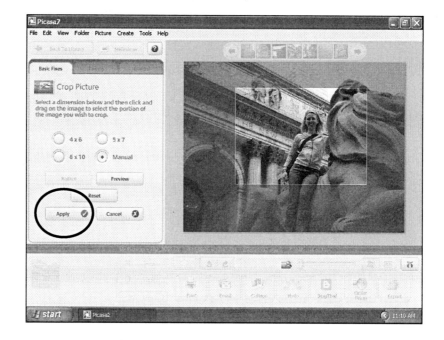

The new cropped picture will appear (bigger) in the window.

Final Step: Click the BACK TO LIBRARY button to return to your pictures.

Your new cropped picture will be saved automatically in the library.

Undoing Changes

A great feature in Picassa is the *Undo* option. The Undo option allows you to go back at least one step and remove an edit you have made. The Undo option comes in handy when you realize you made a mistake or when you change your mind about an edit.

Even after you have exited Picassa, the program will remember the *last* edit performed on each picture and will allow you to Undo it when you reopen Picassa. If you have made edits to five pictures and close Picasso, you can select each picture and Undo the last edit you made to each one, but only the **last** edit. If you cropped a picture, didn't like the way it looked and cropped it again, only the final change can be undone using this feature.

NOTE: Remember, there is an original copy of each picture in your My Pictures Folder. If you make too many changes to a picture, the Undo option may not work. If Undo will not work, you have to opportunity to re-import the original picture and try to edit it again.

Undoing a Change: Step-by-Step Instructions
1. **Double click the image to open the picture, if it is not already open.**
2. **Click the Undo button.**

Undoing a Change: Visual Guide

If you crop a picture and do not like the changes, the changes can be undone by using the UNDO button.

Step One: Double click on the edited picture to open it if it is not already open.

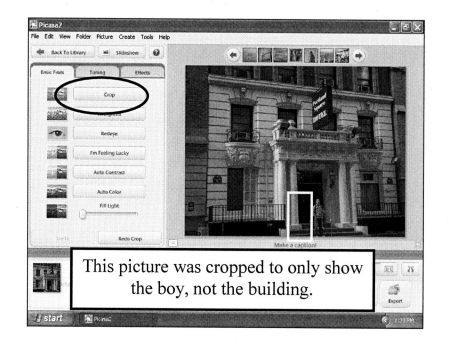

This picture was cropped to only show the boy, not the building.

**Step Two:
Click on the
UNDO button.**

**The change
will
automatically
be reversed
and shown in
the window.**

**In this
example, the
picture was
un-cropped.**

Redoing Changes

In the same manner that the UNDO button removes an unwanted function, REDO reapplies the function. This button can only be used after you have used the UNDO potion. Only the very *last* function that was undone will be redone.

Redoing a Change: Step-by-Step Instructions

1. Double click the image to open the picture, if it is not already open.
2. Click the Redo button.

Redoing a Change: Visual Guide

Once a function has been undone, using UNDO, a REDO button is available.

Step One: If the picture is not already open, double click to open it.

Step Two: Click REDO.

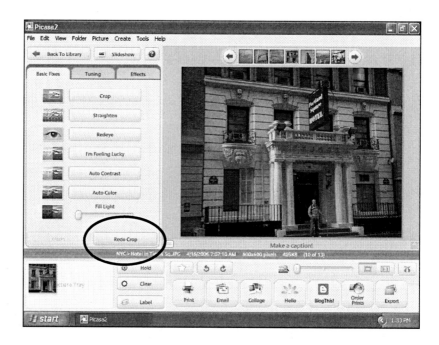

The change will automatically be reversed and shown in the window.

In this case the picture was re-cropped.

Renaming a Picture or File In Picassa

The computer automatically names images when they are transferred from your camera. These names are made up of number and letter sequences that do not make much sense to most users. For example, the name may be automatically stored as A-00001.

Typically, you want to name pictures according to the contents of the picture. For example, you might name the following picture "golf outing." You should use a name that reminds you of the image's content.

Golf Outing

It is best to rename a file using the My Pictures folder, rather than Picassa, although both methods are available. The reason for using the My Pictures folder is that it allows you to immediately see the change, whereas Picassa does not make the name change obvious.

However, the steps for both methods are included in this book. The *Renaming a Picture (Using the My Pictures Folder)* section appears in the chapter on using the My Pictures folder.

Renaming a picture using Picassa **does** also change the name of the picture in the My Pictures folder. It simply isn't immediately recognizable in Picassa because Picassa does not noticeably display picture names. You can look in the My Pictures folder to see the change.

Renaming a Picture in Picassa: Step-by-Step Instructions
1. **Click once on the picture to highlight it.**
2. **Click on the FILE menu.**
3. **Click on RENAME.**
4. **Type in the new name in the text box.**
5. **Click the RENAME button in the window.**
   - **The picture name will be changed in the My Pictures folder and will appear under the picture in Picassa.**

Renaming a Picture in Picassa: Visual Guide

Step One:
Click once on a file that you would like to rename.

Step Two:
Click once on the FILE menu.

Step Three: Select RENAME from the menu.

A Rename Files box will appear displaying the numeric name for the file.

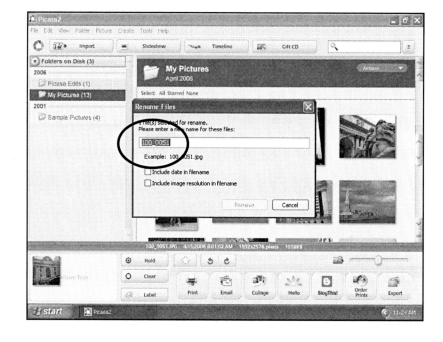

Step Four:
Type a new name in the file box.

Hint: Use a name that applies to the picture's contents.

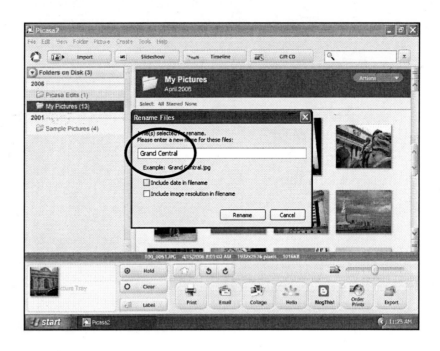

Step Five:
Click on the RENAME button.

In Picassa, the file name will appear only when the picture is selected.

The filename will also automatically be changed in the My Pictures folder, which you will learn to navigate soon.

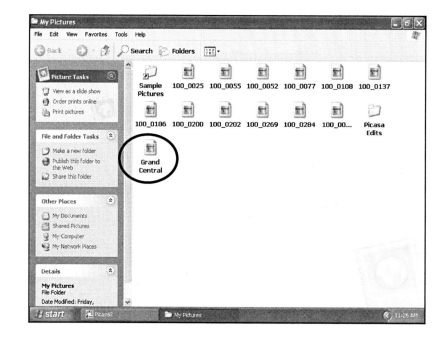

Chapter 14: Photo Editing

Changing the Appearance of a Picture Using Picassa

Photo editing software provides several options for changing the appearance of a picture. Most programs give you the ability to increase or decrease color, brightness, and shadows.

As you've learned, cropping is one way to change the appearance. In this section, you'll learn how to change the color and brightness of the pictures using Picassa's Tuning feature. Picassa allows you to specifically change the fill light, highlights, shadows, and color temperature using the Tuning feature.

Changing the Appearance of a Picture in Picassa: Step-by-Step Instructions

1. Double click to open a picture you would like to change.
2. Click on the TUNING tab to open the tuning tools.
3. Note the slide controls for Fill Light, Highlights, Shadows, and Color Temperature.
4. Slide the control for Fill Light while watching the picture. Stop when the picture appearance seems best.
5. Slide the control for Highlights while watching the picture. Stop when the picture appearance seems best.
6. Slide the control for Shadows while watching the picture. Stop when the picture appearance seems best.
7. Slide the control for Color Temperature while watching the picture. Stop when the picture appearance seems best.
8. Click the BACK TO LIBRARY button to return to your picture list. The changes will be saved automatically.

Changing the Appearance of a Picture in Picassa: Visual Guide

Step One:
Double click to open the picture you would like to change.

Step Two:
Click on the TUNING tab to open the tuning tools.

Step Three: Note the slide controls for Fill Light, Highlights, Shadows, and Color Temperature.

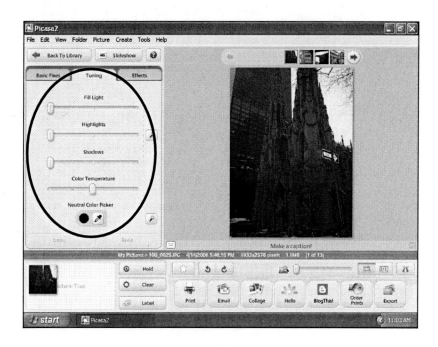

Step Four: Slide the control for Fill Light while watching the picture. Stop when the picture appearance seems best.

Step Five:
Slide the control for Highlights while watching the picture. Stop when the picture appearance seems best.

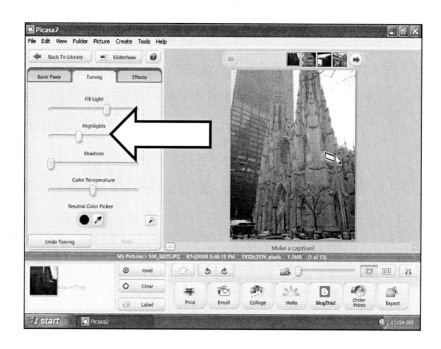

Step Six:
Slide the control for Shadows while watching the picture. Stop when the picture appearance seems best.

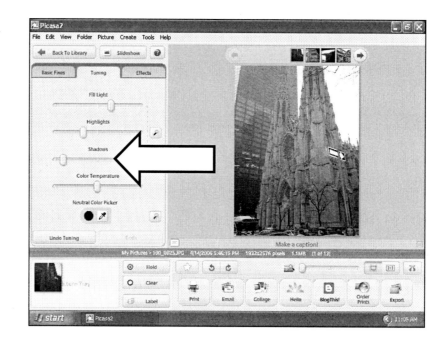

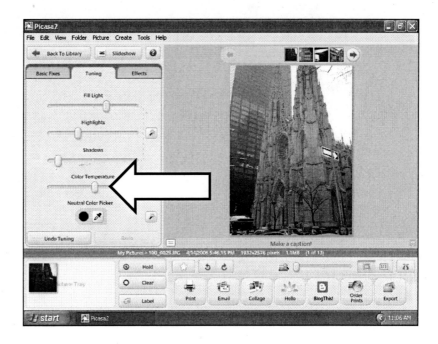

Step Seven:
Slide the control for Color Temperature, while watching the picture. Stop when the picture appearance seems best.

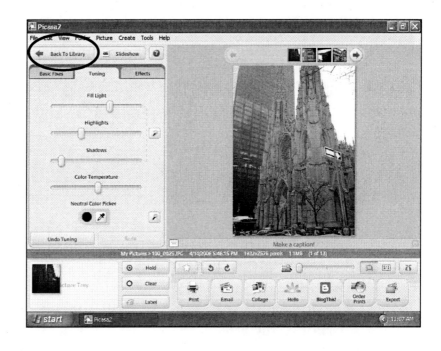

Step Eight:
Click the BACK TO LIBRARY button to return to your picture list.

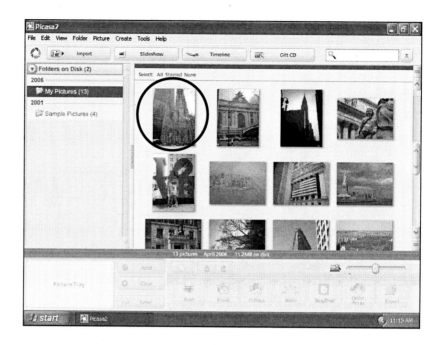

The changed picture will be saved automatically in the Picassa program.

Adding Effects to a Picture using Picassa

Most photo editing programs give users the ability to add effects to pictures, in addition to cropping and changing the appearance. Picassa allows users to make several changes to the picture using the Effects feature.

Picassa's effects include adding Tint, Glow, Black and White, Sepia, and Soft Focus. This section will illustrate how to add the Soft Focus feature to a picture in Picassa.

Adding Effects in Picassa: Step-by-Step Instructions

1. **Double click to open the picture to which you want to add an effect.**
2. **Click on the EFFECTS tab.**
   - **The effects pane will appear.**
3. **Choose the desired effect by clicking once on the name of the effect (Soft Focus).**
   - **The additional features pane will appear allowing you to add to or reduce the effect.**
4. **Click the APPLY button to add the effect.**
5. **Click the YES button to confirm the change.**
6. **Click the BACK TO LIBRARY button to view all pictures. The changes will be saved automatically.**

Chapter 14: Photo Editing

Adding Effects in Picassa: Visual Guide

**Step One:
Double click to
open the
picture to
which you
want to add an
effect.**

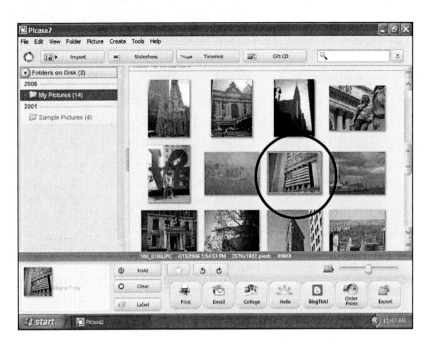

**Step Two:
Click on the
EFFECTS tab.**

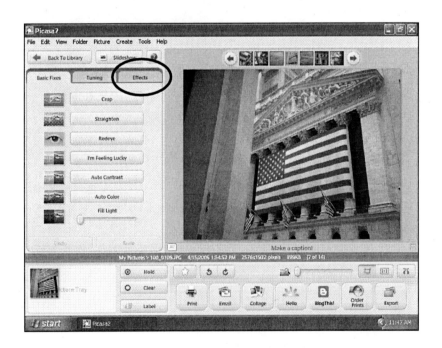

The effects
pane will
appear.

Step Three:
Choose the
desired effect
by clicking once
on the name of
the effect (Soft
Focus).

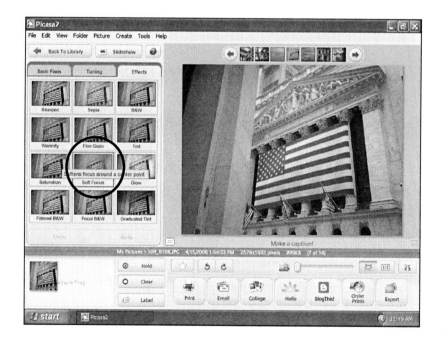

The *additional features* pane will appear allowing you to add to or reduce the effect.

Step Four: Click the APPLY button to add the effect.

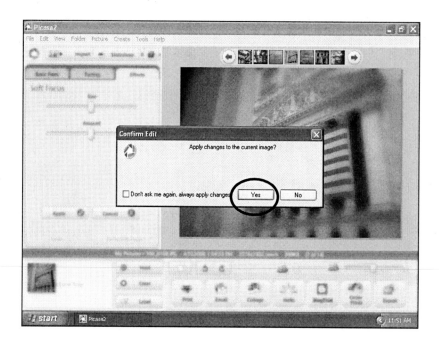

**Step Five:
Click the YES
button to
confirm the
change.**

**Step Six:
Click the
BACK TO
LIBRARY
button to view
all pictures.**

**The changes
will be saved
automatically.**

You have now completed the process of changing the effects of a picture using the Picassa program. Great job!

Chapter 14: Photo Editing

Reducing Red Eye

Another advantage of taking pictures using a digital camera is that you can reduce or even eliminate the "red eye" that seems to appear so often in pictures. Once a picture is taken on your digital camera and transferred to Picassa, you may reduce the red eye found in pictures.

Red eye is caused by a camera's flash illuminating the blood vessels in the back of the eye. Red eye primarily appears in pictures taken from the front of an individual. The red color seems to take over the natural eye color, sacrificing the quality of the picture.

Reducing Red Eye in Pictures: Step-by-Step Instructions

1. **Double click on the picture that has red eye.**
2. **Click on the REDEYE button.**
3. **Place your mouse pointer at the top-left of the eye to start clicking and dragging.**
4. **Click and drag (down and to the right) to cover the red portion of the eye. The red eye will be reduced.**
5. **If needed, repeat step four to fix the other eye. The red eye will be reduced.**
6. **Click the APPLY button. The changes will be applied. Repeat as necessary.**
7. **Click the BACK TO LIBRARY button to return to all pictures.**

Reducing Red Eye in Pictures: Visual Guide

Step One:
Double click on
the picture that
has red eye.

Step Two:
Click on the
REDEYE
button.

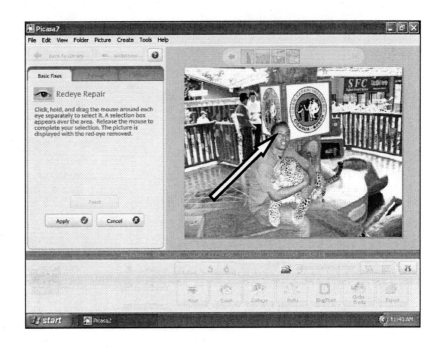

Step Three: Place your mouse pointer at a point to the top-left of the eye.

Step Four: Click and drag (down and to the right) to cover the red portion of the eye. The red eye will be reduced.

Step Five:
If needed,
repeat step
four to fix the
other eye. The
red eye will be
reduced.

Step Six:
Click the
APPLY button.
The changes
will be applied.

Repeat as
necessary.

Step Seven: Click the BACK TO LIBRARY button to return to all pictures.

Your changes will be saved automatically.

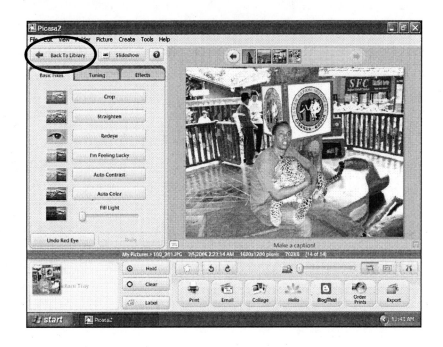

You have now completed the process of reducing red eye on a picture using the Picassa program. Congratulations!

Section 30: Saving Pictures in Picassa

Saving is an important part of working with any photo editing program. Saving allows you to make changes to pictures and then save those changes in two ways:

1. Save changes over the original picture.
2. Save changes separately, which allows you to keep the original and the edited (or altered) picture.

Picassa makes the saving process almost foolproof for users of the program. Picassa makes it difficult for you to lose an original picture, which is a good feature for beginners. This allows you to learn how to edit and save freely, without the worry of accidentally losing the original picture.

Important Notes on the Saving Process in Picassa:

- A copy of each <u>original</u> picture is automatically stored in the MY PICTURES folder when pictures are transferred from your digital camera.
- When first opening Picassa, the program automatically pulls (or imports) a <u>copy</u> of each picture in the MY PICTURES folder to use for editing. This is only a copy. The originals stay unchanged in the MY PICTURES folder.
- Pictures edited in the Picassa program are automatically saved in Picassa after edits are made.
- Intentionally deleting a picture is the only way to lose a picture.
- To get the edited or changed pictures back to the MY PICTURES folder from Picassa, you must export them. Exporting is a process that will be explained later in the book.

The next page shows a chart illustrating how multiple copies of a picture are saved automatically using Picassa.

Originals pictures are <u>manually</u> transferred from digital camera to the **My Pictures Folder.**

Originals are <u>automatically</u> copied into **Picassa** when Picassa is opened. Editing and changes completed here.

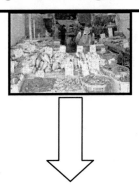

Using Picassa's EXPORT feature, altered pictures are <u>manually</u> exported back to **My Pictures Folder** after edits are made.

The **My Pictures Folder** now contains both the edited & original pictures.

Saving Changes in Picassa

As shown on the previous chart, once you alter an image in Picassa and then return to the picture library, the altered image is immediately saved over the original in the Picassa program.

This means that the picture will automatically be saved, with changes, in Picassa. However, as mentioned earlier, an original, unchanged copy of the picture remains in the My Pictures folder. This is a great feature for beginning users.

Saving Changes over an Original Picture in Picassa: Step-by-Step Instructions

1. Open a picture to edit.
2. Make edits as necessary to a picture.
3. Make sure you are satisfied with the changes you have made.
4. Click on the BACK TO LIBRARY button in Picassa. Your changes have been saved in the Picassa program automatically. (An original, unchanged picture will still exist in the My Pictures folder)

Saving Changes in Picassa: Visual Guide

Step One:
Open a
picture to
edit.

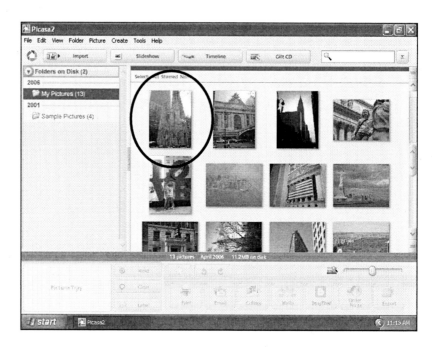

Step Two: Make changes as necessary to the picture.

Experiment with the slides to brighten the picture.

Step Three: Complete the edits or changes to the picture. Make sure you are satisfied with the picture.

Step Four: Click the BACK TO LIBRARY button.

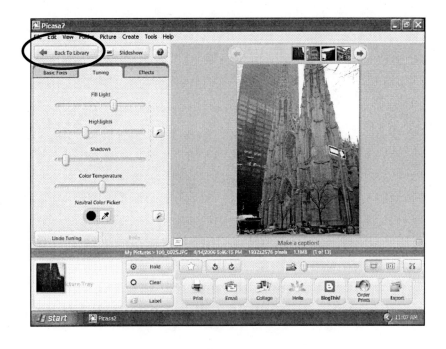

The picture
will
automatically
be saved, with
changes, in the
Picassa library.

Saving Options in Picassa

When saving a picture in Picassa, you have two options. First, you can save your changed picture. This means that the only copy of the picture in Picassa will be the changed/edited photograph. A second option is to save a copy of the picture so that you can make edits to one picture and also leave an original, unchanged picture in the Picassa program. This will give you two pictures, one original photo and one edited photo.

Making a Copy of a Picture in Picassa: Step-by-Step Instructions

1. Open a picture to edit and save.
2. Make changes as necessary (in Picassa, you must make at least one small change or edit to be able to save a copy of a file).
3. Click on the FILE menu and choose SAVE A COPY option.
4. Click the BACK TO LIBRARY button.
5. A second copy of the picture, as displayed, will be saved in the Picassa program, as well as in the MY PICTURES folder.

Chapter 14: Photo Editing

Making a Copy of a Picture in Picassa: Visual Guide

Step One:
Open an Image
to Edit and
Save.

Step Two:
Make any
changes or
edits necessary.

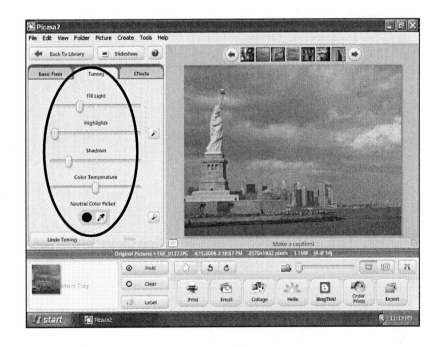

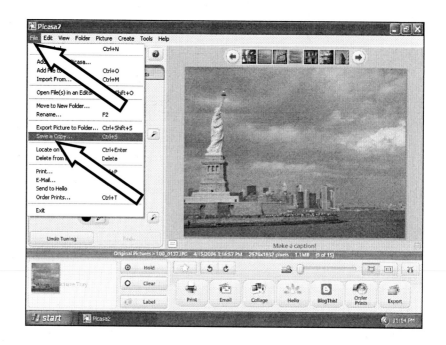

Step Three:
Click on the
FILE menu and
choose the
SAVE A COPY
option.

Step Four:
Click the BACK
TO LIBRARY
button.

Two copies will now exist within the Picassa program.

You may now make changes to one copy and keep the other (original copy) unchanged.

You have now successfully completed the process of making a copy of a picture in Picassa. Terrific work!

Important Points related to Making a Copy of a Picture before Making Changes

- Making copies is a great way for Beginners to experiment with the editing process. It is strongly recommended that you make a copy after editing a picture.
- Making a copy of an image before making changes will insure that you do not accidentally, but permanently, alter your original.
- After making a copy, you can always return to your original print.
- You can make a copy by selecting SAVE A COPY or SAVE AS option.

Section 31: Desktop Pictures

Replacing your Computer's Wallpaper with your Picture

The picture that appears when you first start your computer, before you have opened any programs or windows, is typically referred to as your desktop. This image is also known as the wallpaper or the background. Therefore, depending on who you are talking to, this picture may be referred to as the desktop, background, or wallpaper.

The wallpaper is traditionally set using the computer's CONTROL PANEL. Using the CONTROL PANEL allows you to choose from a predetermined list of wallpaper pictures. However, if you want to use a picture you have taken as your desktop, the process is a little different.

In this exercise, you will replace your wallpaper with a picture you have taken with your digital camera.

Changing your Computer's Wallpaper to a Picture You Have Taken (Using Picassa): Step-by-Step Instructions

1. **Open Picassa using the Start menu.**
2. **Find the picture you would like to use as your wallpaper.**
3. **Double click on the picture to open it.**
4. **Click on the CREATE menu.**
5. **Select the SET AS DESKTOP option from the menu.**
6. **Answer YES to the confirmation question.**
7. **Close all windows to see your new desktop picture.**

Changing your Computer's Wallpaper to a Picture You Have Taken (Using Picassa): Visual Guide

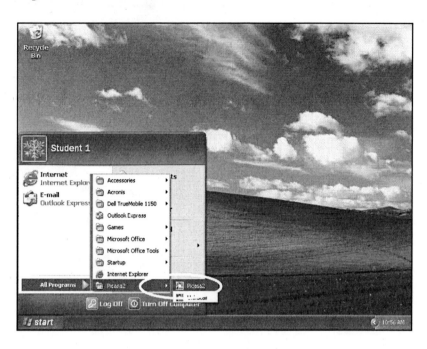

Step One:
Open Picassa using the START menu.

Step Two:
Find the picture you would like to use as your wallpaper.

Step Three:
Double click on the picture to open it.

Step Four:
Click on the
CREATE
menu.

Step Five:
Click on the
SET AS
DESKTOP
option from the
menu.

Step Six: Click on the YES button.

Step Seven: Close the window using the "X" in the upper right corner.

Your new background picture will appear on the computer's desktop!

Section 32: Exporting Pictures

One benefit to using Picassa is that, as you edit and change your pictures, the original unchanged pictures remain in the My Pictures folder. This is a benefit to beginners who don't want to chance losing the original picture as they learn how to edit and save. In essence, you'll always have a backup picture in the My Pictures folder.

Again, keeping the originals in the My Pictures folder is an advantage for beginners. Having multiple copies of your picture only presents an issue when you want to email a picture that you have changed or edited. In order to email your changed pictures, Picassa users need to get the changed or edited pictures into the My Pictures folder.

Chapter 14: Photo Editing

You must use the EXPORT feature in the Picassa program to get the changed or edited pictures from Picassa to the My Pictures folder. This will give you the ability to attach the pictures to an email. (Attaching pictures to emails will be covered in the next section).

NOTE: Many other photo editing programs make changes to the actual picture in the My Pictures folder. These programs give you the option to save your changes over the original picture or save the changes you've made as a new file in the My Pictures folder. If this is the case for the photo editing software you are using, you do not need to export the pictures.

Exporting Pictures in Picassa: Step-by-Step Instructions

1. **Open Picassa and locate the pictures you would like to export.**
2. **To select all the pictures to export, click on the ALL button.**
    a. **All the pictures in that folder will be selected (will become outlined in blue).**
    b. **To select a single picture to export, simply click once to highlight that particular picture.**
3. **Click on EXPORT at the bottom right corner of the window.**
    - **Picassa automatically exports to the MY Pictures folder unless you specify otherwise. The location is shown under "Location of exported folder."**
4. **Change the size of the exported pictures by moving the *pixels* slide to the left or right.**
    - **If you want to email the pictures, it is recommended that you select the smallest size available by moving the image size slide to the far left.**
5. **Move the *image quality* slide to the far right to maximize the quality of the pictures.**
    - **Moving the quality slide to the far right is the best option to preserve the quality of the picture.**
6. **Type the name of the new folder that will house the exported pictures.**
    - **Use a name that indicates what is in the folder, such as "vacation pictures," or "wedding."**
7. **Click on the OK button.**

- The edited pictures will be exported (copied) to the My Pictures folder. The status bar will indicate when this process has been completed.

8. Close the pop-up window that appears confirming the export.

Export Pictures in Picassa: Visual Guide

Step One:
Open Picassa and locate the pictures you would like to export.

Step Two:
To select all of the pictures in Picassa for exporting, click on the (very small) ALL button.

If you only want to export one picture, click on that picture. It will be outlined in blue.

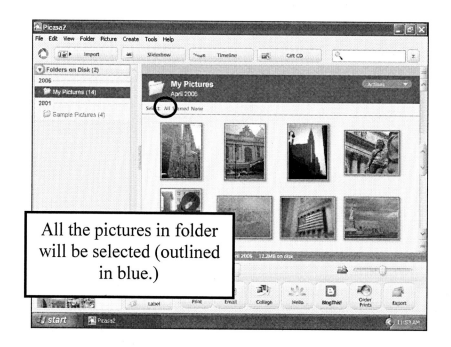

All the pictures in folder will be selected (outlined in blue.)

Step Three:
Click the
EXPORT
button in the
bottom right
corner of the
window.

Step Four:
Change the size
of the exported
pictures by
moving the
pixels **slide to**
the left or
right.

NOTE: If you are going to email these pictures, move the slide to the far left. This will reduce the picture size. Some picture quality may be lost, but it will take up far less space on the computer and will take less time to attach.

Step Five:
Move the
image quality
slide to the far
right to
maximize the
quality of the
pictures.

Step Six:
Type the name
of the new
folder that will
contain the
exported
pictures.

**Step Seven:
Click on the
OK button.**

**The edited
pictures will be
exported
(copied) to the
My Pictures
folder. The
status bar will
indicate when
this process has
been
completed.**

Step Eight: Close the pop-up window that appears, using the "X" in the upper, right corner of the Picassa Exports window.

Printing Pictures

By now, you have learned a great deal about your digital camera. You have learned how to take pictures, transfer pictures, and save pictures onto your computer. Next, you will learn how to print your pictures.

For many people, a major motivation of using a digital camera is to be able to share pictures with family and friends. Printing is one very popular way to share your pictures.

Printing pictures is relatively easy in the Picassa program. The program allows you to choose the size of the picture and the number of copies to print. Printing pictures from the My Pictures folder will be discussed later.

Printing Pictures in Picassa: Step-by-Step Instructions
1. In Picassa, open the image you would like to print.
2. Click on the FILE menu, and select the PRINT option.
3. Select the size of picture you want to print. Do this by clicking on the button indicating the size you want.
4. Choose the number of copies you wish to print.
5. Click on the PRINT button in the bottom right corner of the window.

Printing a Picture in Picassa: (Visual Guide)

Step One:
In Picassa, open the picture by double clicking on it.

Step Two:
Click on your FILE menu, and select PRINT.

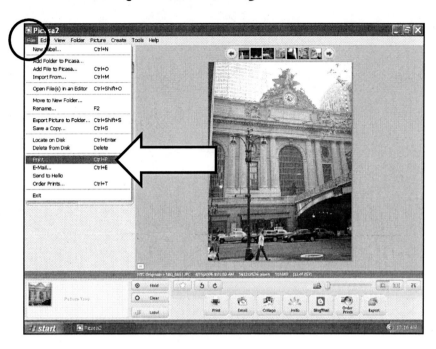

A print pane will open on the left side of the window.

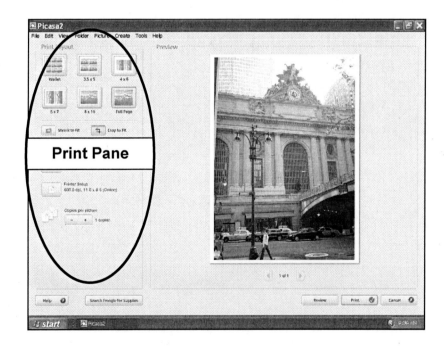

Step Three:
Select the size
of picture you
want to print.
Do this by
clicking on the
button
indicating the
size you want.

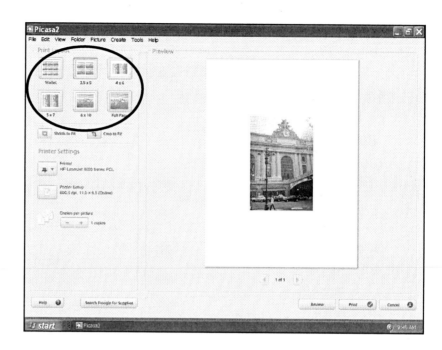

Step Four:
Choose the
number of
copies you wish
to print.
Increase or
decrease the
number by
using the + and
– buttons.

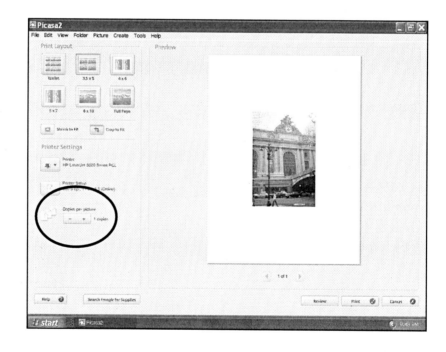

Step Five:
Click on the
PRINT button
in the bottom
right corner of
the window.

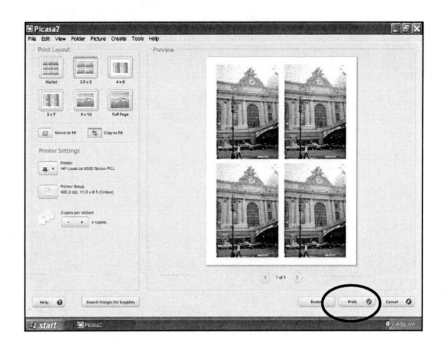

Chapter 15

Working in the My Pictures Folder

What You Will Learn in This Chapter:
- ✓ Accessing the My Pictures Folder
- ✓ Viewing different icons in the My Pictures Folder
- ✓ Opening a Picture in the My Pictures Folder
- ✓ Renaming a Picture in the My Pictures Folder
- ✓ Deleting a Picture in the My Pictures Folder

Chapter 15: Working in the My Pictures Folder

What is the My Pictures Folder?

The My Pictures folder is a Windows-provided folder to which you can save your pictures. My Pictures is, in essence, a reserved space on the computer's hard drive for your pictures. All computers have a My Pictures folder, which makes it easy to find and work with pictures.

Not only are you able to put pictures in the My Pictures folder, the folder will automatically retain a copy of any picture transferred to your computer from a digital camera. This is the reason the My Pictures folder is so important. At least one copy of every digital picture will be in this folder, regardless of whether you put it there or not.

By now you are familiar with Picassa and the power it gives you to collect your pictures, edit them, and export them back to the My Pictures folder. As you have learned, Picassa is great for these tasks.

To organize what you have created, you now want to access and use the My Pictures folder. The My Pictures folder allows you to perform several tasks to organize your pictures. Some of these tasks, such as renaming, deleting, and viewing pictures can also be performed in the Picassa program.

When you have worked with both processes, you will learn that Picassa is a better choice to edit pictures, while the My Pictures folder is better suited for organizing pictures.

This section will review various ways to organize picture files on your computer using the My Pictures folder.

Section 33: Accessing My Pictures

Accessing My Pictures: Step-by-Step Instructions
1. Click on START.
2. Click on MY PICTURES.
   - The My Pictures folder will open.

Accessing My Pictures: Visual Guide

Step One:
Click on
START.

Step Two:
Click on MY
PICTURES.

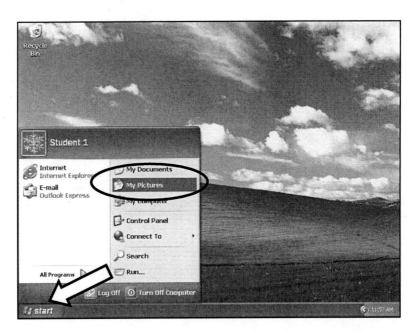

Changing the View of Picture Files in the My Pictures Folder
You may select one of several options to view pictures or icons in the My Pictures folder. You can choose the size and the amount of descriptive data you will see. If you choose an icon view, the picture image itself does not appear. A picture file is represented when the icon (to the right) is displayed.

173

Your choices of icon views include:
- Filmstrip
- Thumbnails
- Tiles
- Icons
- List
- Details

A description of each view:

Filmstrip: Shows pictures in a linear order. It allows you to choose which pictures you want to display in a slideshow format. You can move through the pictures by using the arrow keys on your keyboard. Filmstrip view is the best option for showing your pictures to other people.

Thumbnails: Allows you to view a small or condensed replica of the actual picture. Thumbnails allow you to get a quick overview of each picture without having to open it.

Tiles: Displays full-sized picture icons. In tile view, you cannot see a picture unless you open the file.

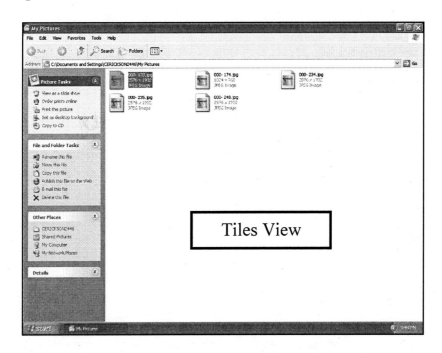

Icons: Displays medium-sized picture icons. This setting displays more picture files in a single window which limits scrolling. In this view, you cannot see a picture unless you open the file.

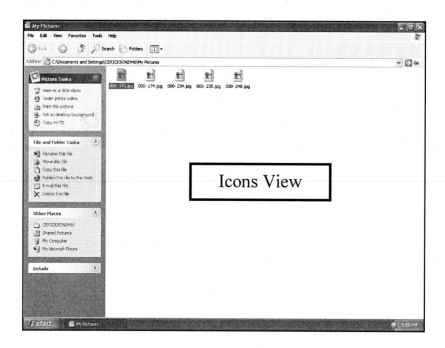

List: Displays small-sized picture icons. This setting allows the most picture files to fit in a single window which limits scrolling. In this view, you cannot see a picture unless you open the file.

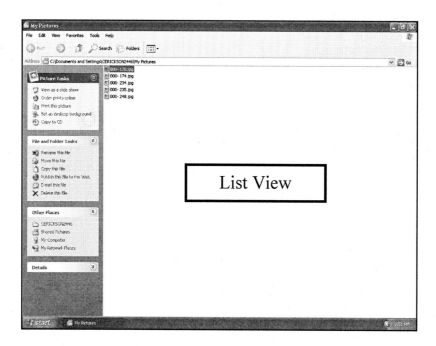

Details: Shows small-sized icons. Detail view gives details of each picture file including the size, the type, the date modified, the date taken, and the dimensions. In this view, you cannot see a picture unless you open the file.

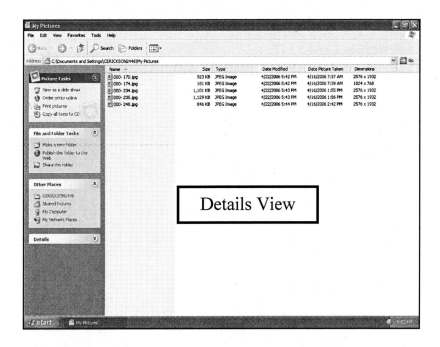

Changing the View of Picture Files: Step-by-Step Instructions
1. **Click on the START button.**
2. **Click on the MY PICTURES option.**
3. **Click on the VIEW Menu.**
4. **Select one of the six views by clicking once on the preferred view.**

Changing the View of Picture Files: Visual Guide

Step One: Click the START button.

Step Two: Click on the MY PICTURES option.

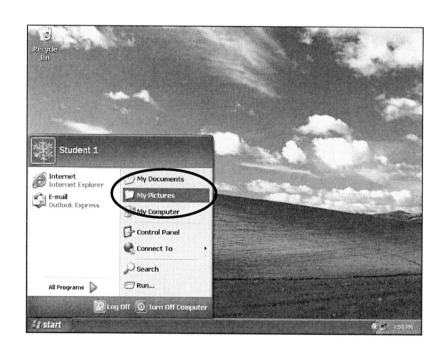

**Step Three:
Click on the
VIEW
Menu**

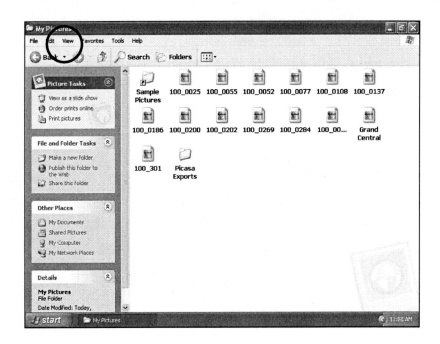

**Step Four:
Select one of
the six views
by clicking
once on the
preferred
view.**

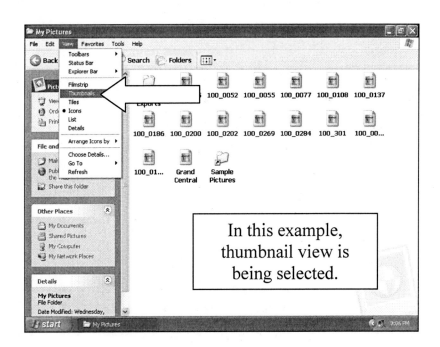

In this example,
thumbnail view is
being selected.

The selected view will change the appearance of the picture files.

Here, thumbnail view is displayed.

Section 34: Organizing Pictures by Creating Folders (In the My Pictures Folder)

As you become more familiar with your digital camera and photo editing, you will accumulate pictures on your computer. Computers can hold thousands of pictures and have become the primary storage location for pictures.

Think of your computer as the large box (you usually keep in the spare bedroom) full of all the pictures you have developed over the years. The box contains pictures from dozens, maybe hundreds, or even thousands of events you have attended.

The great thing about having your pictures on your computer, as opposed to the big box in the bedroom, is that you can easily organize the pictures as you store them. A computer is a great way to organize pictures from all types of events.

Chapter 15: Working in the My Pictures Folder

One of the best ways to organize your pictures on your computer is with folders. The computer lets you create new folders whenever you want. So for you neat nicks, you're in luck!

The process of organizing pictures into folders includes two major steps: First, an empty folder must be created. Next, the pictures must be put into the folder. Sounds easy, right? It is. Let's get started!

Creating an Empty Folder (In the My Pictures Folder): Step-by-Step Instructions

1. **Click the FILE menu.**
2. **Move down to the NEW option.**
3. **Slide the arrow across to the submenu and click on FOLDER.**
   a. **A new folder will be created. It is <u>waiting to be named</u>.**
   b. **Do not click with the mouse again.**
4. **Type the name of the folder. The name will be placed under the folder.**
5. **Press the ENTER key on the keyboard.**

Creating an Empty Folder (In the My Documents Folder): Visual Guide

**Step One:
Click the
FILE menu.**

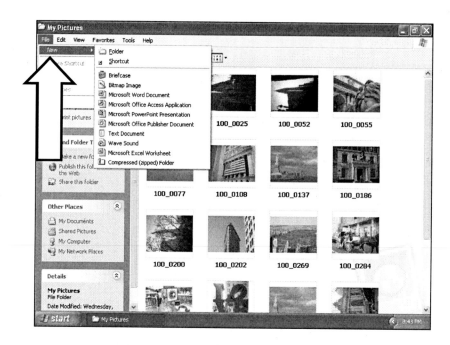

**Step Two:
Move down
to the NEW
option.**

**Step Three:
Slide the
arrow
across to the
submenu
and click on
FOLDER.**

A new folder
will be
created. __It is
waiting to be
named.__

Do not click
with the
mouse again.

Step Four:
Type the
name of the
folder. The
name will be
placed under
the folder.

This folder
has been titled
"Original
Pictures."

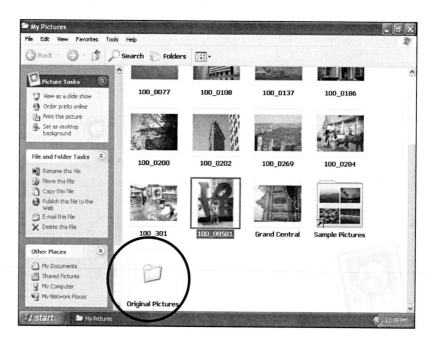

Step Five: Press the ENTER key on the keyboard.

You have now created your own folder for pictures. Organization is only a few steps away!

Moving Pictures into Folders

Now that you have created an empty folder, the next step is to fill it with pictures. Filling a folder with pictures is easy and fun, really!

All you have to do to put any picture into the folder is drag and drop the picture. Remember, dragging and dropping is a movement with the mouse in which you click on the object (picture) that you wish to move, hold the mouse button down, drag the object to the target (the folder), and then let go of the mouse button.

Once you have dragged and dropped the first picture, continue dragging and dropping pictures into the new folder until you have moved all the pictures into that particular folder.

Moving a Picture into a Folder: Step-by-Step Instructions

1. **Click on the picture you want to move, and hold the mouse button down.**
2. **Move the mouse toward the folder into which you want to move the picture.**
3. **When you reach the folder with the mouse arrow (the folder should become highlighted), release the mouse button. The picture will drop into the folder.**

Moving a Picture into a Folder: Visual Guide

Step One:
Click on the picture you wish to move and hold down the mouse button.

Step Two:
Move the mouse toward the folder into which you want to move the picture.

Step Three:
When you reach the target folder with the mouse arrow (the folder should become highlighted), release the mouse button.

The picture will drop into the folder.

Chapter 15: Working in the My Pictures Folder

Try again with another picture:

Step One: Click on the picture you want to move and hold down the mouse button.

Step Two: Move the mouse toward the folder into which you want to move the picture.

Step Three: When you have reached the target folder with the mouse arrow (the folder should become highlighted), release the mouse button.

The picture will drop into the folder.

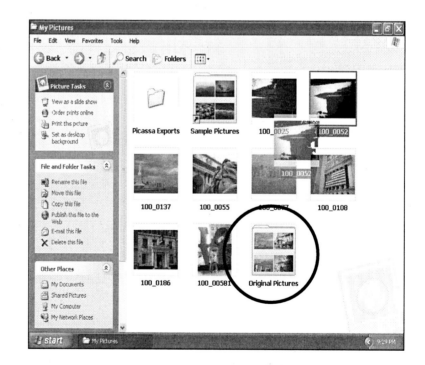

When all of your pictures have been moved, you will be left with folders filled with pictures. To access any picture, double click the folder housing the appropriate group of pictures. The folder will open. Finally, double click on the specific picture.

This view shows what a well organized My Pictures Folder looks like.

To look at the pictures inside any folder, double click on the folder.

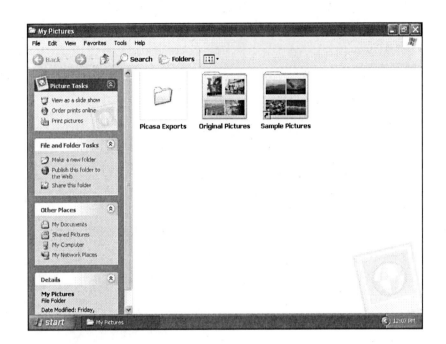

Accessing the Picassa Exports Folder
It is time to organize the pictures exported to the folder. You will access the Picassa Exports folder to see the pictures you edited and exported from Picassa.

Accessing the Picassa Exports Folder: Step-by-Step Directions
1. **Double click on the Picassa Export Folder to open it.**
2. **Double-click on the subfolder, (which you previously named) that contains the pictures you'd like to organize.**

Accessing the Picassa Exports Folder: Visual Guide

Step One: Double-click on the Picassa Exports folder to open it.

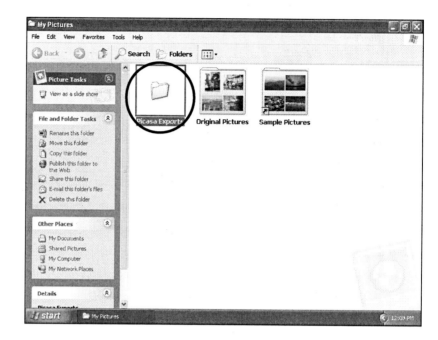

Step Two: Double-click on the subfolder, which you named in the previous section, containing the pictures you'd like to organize.

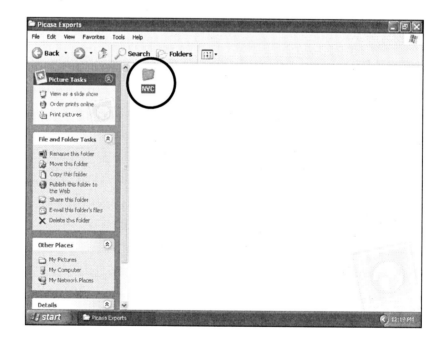

NOTE: Each folder will have a separate, pre-set view. Changing the view to thumbnails in the My Pictures folder does not change the view in all folders. As you continue moving through your folders, you may need to change the view in each of the folders.

The pictures may not be displayed in the view you want.

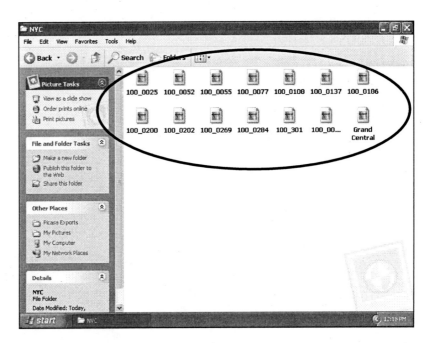

To change the view in any window (Review):

Step One:
Select the
VIEW menu.

Step Two:
Click on
THUMBNAILS
in the menu.

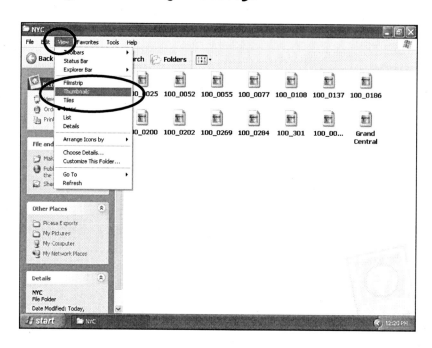

The view has
changed to
Thumbnails.

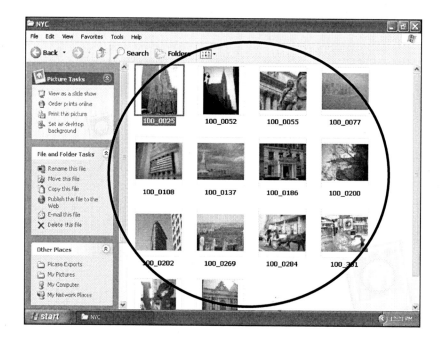

The thumbnail view is useful to help identify pictures that have not yet been renamed. The next section will explain how to select and rename pictures in the My Pictures folder.

Section 35: Functions in the My Documents Folder

Renaming a Picture (Using the My Pictures Folder)

As you learned earlier, you can give pictures file names that correlate to the picture contents. Similar to renaming in Picassa, renaming a picture in My Picture Folder allows you to assign a name that is related to the picture's content. This process will help you manage and organize your pictures as you continue to accumulate pictures on your computer.

Although you learned to rename pictures using Picassa in a previous section, renaming pictures in the My Pictures folder is recommended for beginners.

Why Should You Use the My Pictures Folder to Rename a Picture?

The first reason to use the My Picture Folder to rename pictures is because you can immediately see the name changes. It simplifies the organization process.

A second reason is that renaming a picture file utilizes the same process used to rename any type of computer file. If you are familiar with naming files in other computer programs, renaming a picture file will be simple for you. If you are not familiar with naming files, renaming pictures in My Pictures will help you when you decide to work in other programs. The processes are identical.

The instructions below will walk you through process of renaming a file in the My Pictures folder. As you'll see, the process is easy and the name change is recognizable immediately, unlike Picassa.

Using the thumbnail view aids the process by allowing you to see pictures and assign names without having to open the pictures.

Chapter 15: Working in the My Pictures Folder

Renaming a Picture (In the My Pictures Folder): Step-by-Step Instructions

1. Select a picture to rename by clicking once on the picture. The picture will become highlighted.
2. Click on the FILE menu, move to the RENAME option and click once.
   a. The picture will be ready to be named.
   b. Do not click the mouse again.
3. Type a name for the picture which describes the picture's contents.
   - The name will appear under the picture.
4. Press the ENTER key on the keyboard.

Renaming a Picture (In the My Pictures Folder): Visual Guide

Step One: Select a picture to rename by clicking once on the picture. The picture will become highlighted.

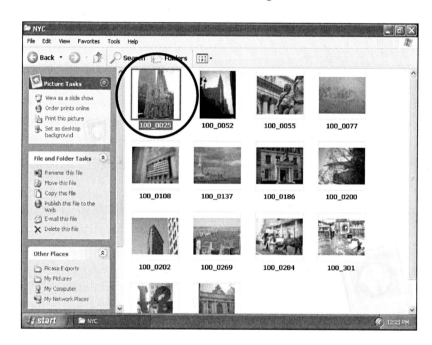

Step Two:
Click on the
FILE menu,
move to the
RENAME
option. Click
one time.

The picture is
ready to be
named.
Do not click
the mouse
again.

Step Three:
Type a name for
the picture
describing the
picture's
contents.

The name you type will automatically appear under the picture.

The name will appear under the picture.

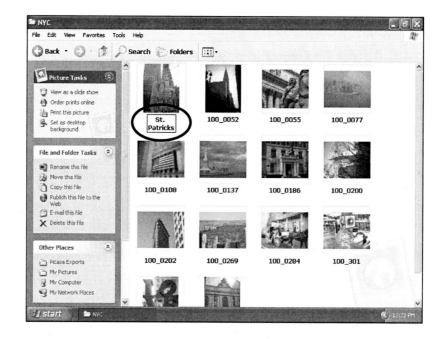

Step Four: Press the ENTER key on the keyboard.

Now, try to name all of the pictures in your folder:

When all the pictures have been renamed, you're one step closer to being completely organized!

Deleting a Picture (in the My Pictures Folder)

Thusfar, there has been no discussion related to deleting pictures from your computer. You've learned how to delete pictures directly from the digital camera. It is just as important to understand how to delete pictures from your computer.

Deleting pictures from the computer helps you get rid of unwanted pictures, such as poor quality, embarrassing, or useless pictures. Remember, with a digital camera you have the power to choose which pictures are printed or shared.

Deleting unwanted pictures from your computer is helpful not only because it removes them from your sight, but also because it opens up valuable hard drive space on your computer. Over time, pictures can take up a significant amount of space. Regularly "throwing out the bad" is a good habit to form.

Deleting Pictures (In the My Pictures Folder): Step-by-Step Instructions

1. Click once on the picture you want to delete.
2. Select the FILE menu and click once on the DELETE option.
3. Confirm deletion by clicking YES.

Deleting Pictures (In the My Pictures Folder): Visual Guide

Step One:

Click once on the picture you want to delete.

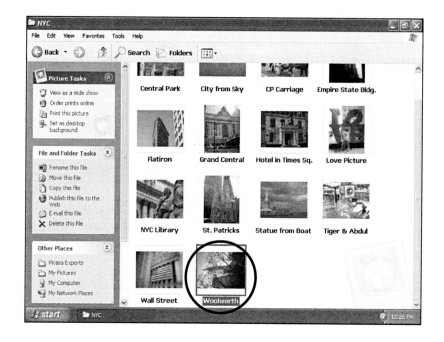

Step Two: Select the FILE menu and click once on DELETE.

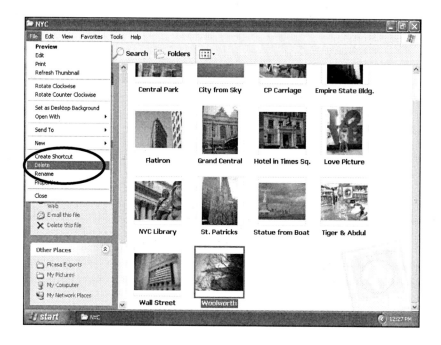

Step Three: Confirm deletion by clicking on YES.

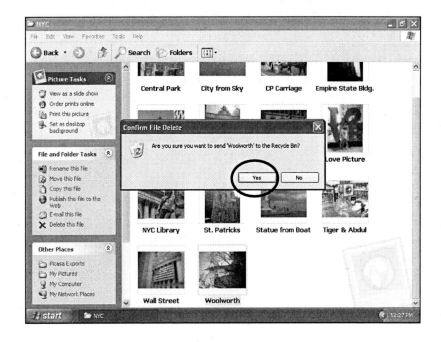

The picture will be removed from the folder.

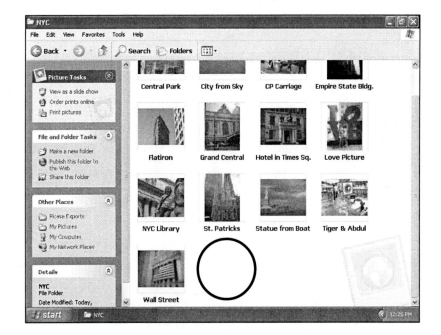

Chapter 15: Working in the My Pictures Folder

<u>Chapter 16</u>

E-mailing Pictures

What You Will Learn in This Chapter:
- ✓ What are attachments?
- ✓ Emailing a picture
- ✓ Receiving an emailed picture
- ✓ Impact of file size on emailed pictures

Chapter 16: E-mailing Pictures

Section 36: Email

A significant advantage of taking pictures digitally is it enables you to share the pictures by email. As you may know, email is a method of communicating on the computer that allows you to send text messages (and pictures) to another person via an email address.

Attachments

Email has become a primary form of communication and is a great way to stay in touch with friends and relatives, both near and far. Although many people use email to simply send text letters to each other, an advanced feature allows you to send a file or picture with the written message. This is known as *sending an attachment.*

Email allows you to electronically send any picture you have taken with your digital camera to other people using their email addresses. Later, when they check their email inboxes, they will see that you sent them a message with an attachment. Upon opening the attachment, they will be able to view the picture you sent.

This section will walk you though the steps to send a picture attachment.

Sending a Picture Attachment by Email: Step-by-Step Instructions

1. **Click on the "CREATE" button (also called "COMPOSE" or "WRITE") located near the top of your email inbox.**
   - **Maximize the window if necessary.**
2. **Type the address of the person you are sending the letter to in the "TO:" field (ex. Jack@aol.com) and type the subject of the letter in the "SUBJECT" box (ex. "vacation pictures").**
3. **Click once in the large writing area and type any message that you want to accompany your picture.**

4. Click on the ATTACH button (or "BROWSE" button.) It may have a picture of a paper clip nearby.
    a. The "Insert Attachment" window will appear.
    b. This screen enables you to search through your computer for the file you want to attach.
5. Click on the VIEWS menu and change the view to THUMBNAILS if it is not already set to thumbnails. If you do not change the view to thumbnails, you may only be able to see file names in the browse window and not the actual pictures.
6. Locate the picture and click on it once.
    a. Locate the file by clicking inside the "Look In:" box and selecting the My Documents folder.
    b. Double click on the My Pictures folder or the folder that contains your picture.
    c. Continue to navigate through any necessary folders by double clicking to look inside the folders, and find the picture.
    d. Click on the picture file one time to highlight the title.
7. Click the ATTACH button.
    a. The file will be attached and the title will appear in the attachment line.
    b. Keep in mind that the computer may take a few minutes to attach the file.
8. Click the SEND button to send the message.

The picture(s) will be sent, along with your email message, to the person whose address you entered in the TO line.

Chapter 16: E-mailing Pictures

Sending a Picture Attachment by Email: Visual Guide

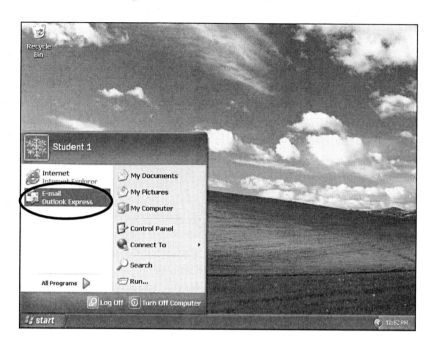

Opening Email:

Follow your normal procedure to open and view your email.

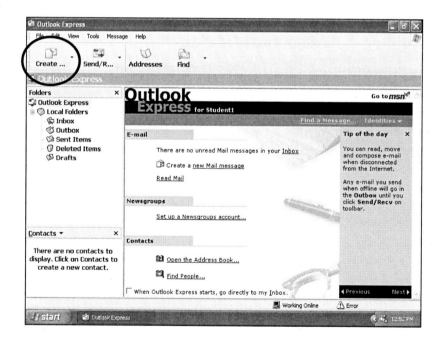

Step One:
Click the CREATE button (may also be called COMPOSE or WRITE) located near the top of your email inbox.

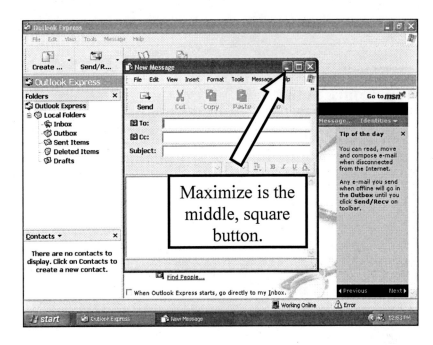

Maximize window if necessary.

Maximize is the middle, square button.

Step Two:
Type the email address of the person you are sending the letter to in the "TO:" field.
Type the subject of the email in the "SUBJECT" field.

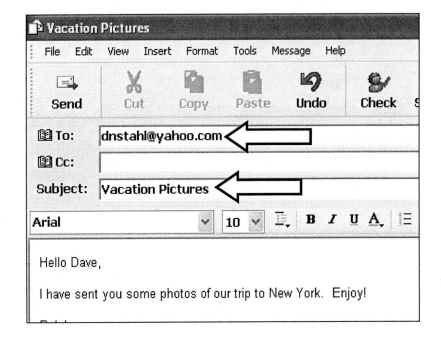

Step Three: Click once in the large writing area and type the message you want to send with your picture.

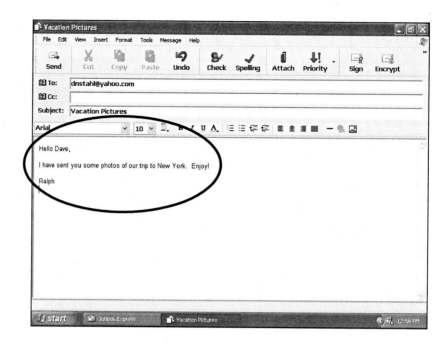

Step Four: Click the ATTACH button (or BROWSE button). It may have a picture of a paper clip nearby.

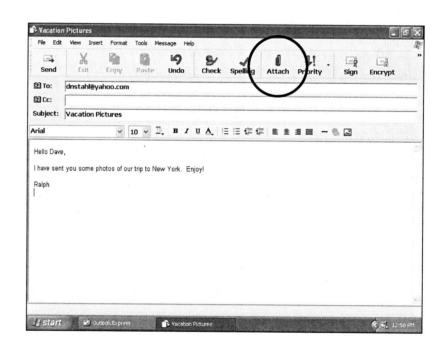

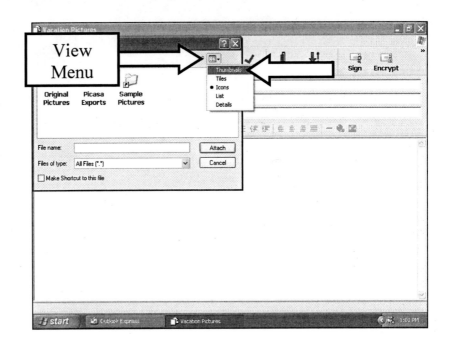

Step Five:
Click on the
VIEWS menu
and change the
view to
THUMBNAILS

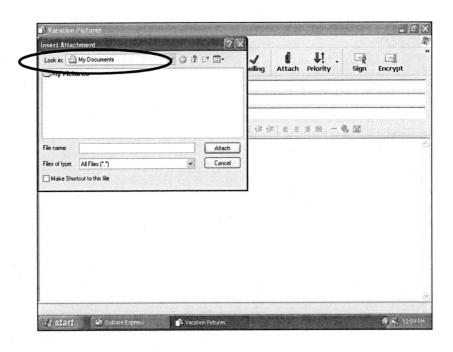

Step 6A:
Locate the file
by clicking
inside the "Look
In:" box and
selecting MY
DOCUMENTS.

Step 6B:
Double click the
MY PICTURES
folder (or the
folder that
contains your
picture).

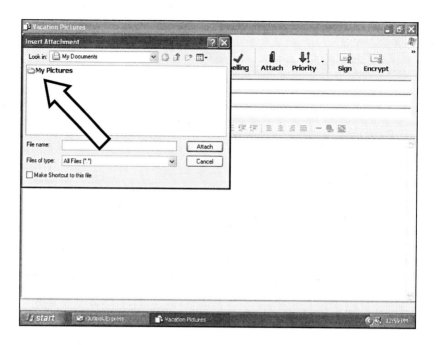

Step 6C:
Continue to
navigate through
any necessary
folders by
double-clicking
to look inside the
folders and find
the picture.

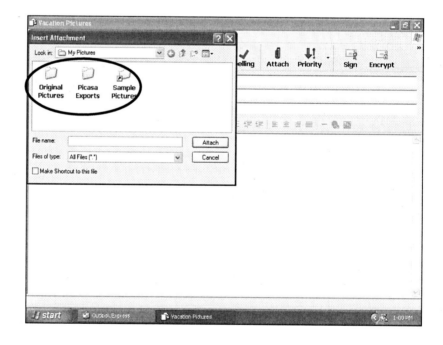

Step 6D:
Click on the
picture file once
to highlight the
title.

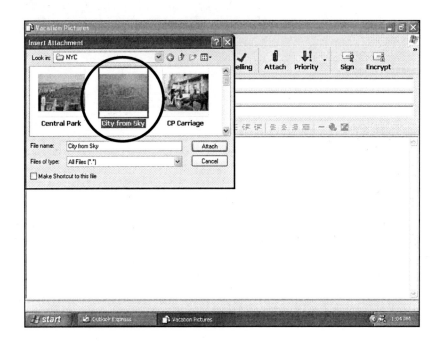

Step Seven:
Click the
ATTACH
button.

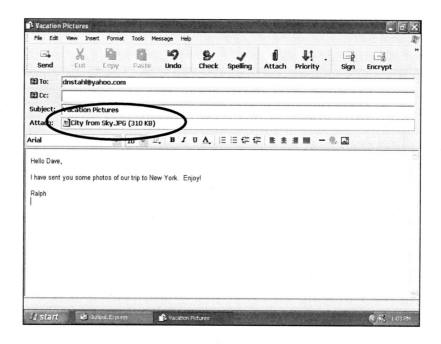

The file will be
attached, and
the title will
appear in the
attachment line.

Step Eight:
Click on the
SEND button to
send the message.

You have now successfully sent a picture by email. Congratulations!

Sending Additional Pictures

In some cases, you may choose to send a second picture in the same email. You can send additional pictures by repeating steps 4-7 before sending the message.

Once you are comfortable with attachments, the process of sending additional pictures in the same email is very simple. Just follow the same steps to add a second attachment.

Attaching a Second Picture before Sending an Email: Step-by-Step Instructions

1. Follow steps 1-7 above to attach a single picture to an email message.
2. Repeat steps 4-7 to attach additional pictures as desired.
3. Click on the SEND button to send the message.

Attaching a Second Picture before Sending an Email: Visual Guide

Step One:
Follow steps 1-7 to attach a single picture to an email message.

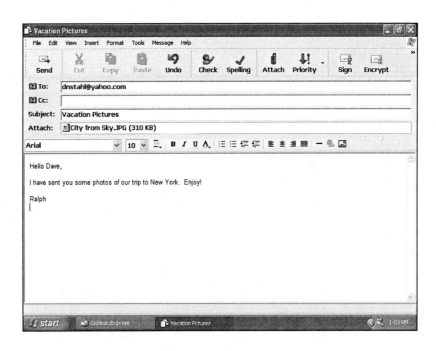

Step Two:
Repeat steps 4-7 to attach additional pictures as desired.

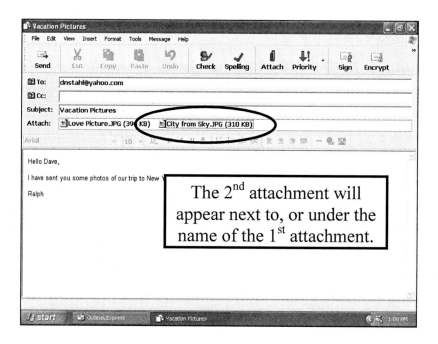

The 2nd attachment will appear next to, or under the name of the 1st attachment.

Step Three:
Click the SEND button to send the message.

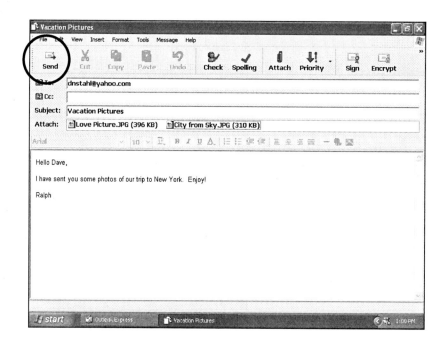

Receipt of an Email with an Attachment

Receipt of an attachment in your email inbox is typically indicated in email by a paperclip symbol, such as the one shown below.

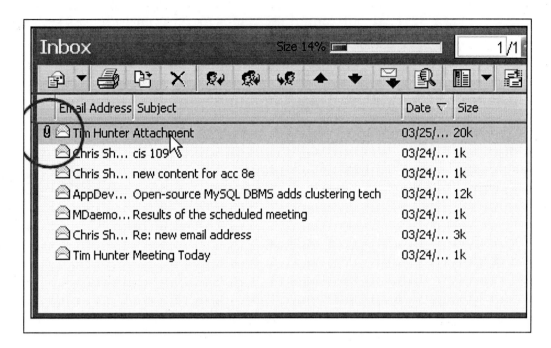

To better understand attachments, think of the process of sending a box or package through standard U.S. Mail as opposed to sending a standard letter. Sending a package takes a few more steps than sending a standard letter. The same is true for attaching a file to an email.

Continue to compare a text email to a standard letter; think of an attachment as a package to be delivered. Just as a package takes more space in a mailbox than a letter does, an email attachment takes more electronic space than an email message does in an email box. This is important because:

1. There is a limit to the size of email that can be sent, determined by your specific email service.
2. There is a limit to the amount of space that recipients have in their email boxes to receive and store messages, determined by their specific email service.

When sending an email attachment, it is important to be aware of the size of the 'package' you are sending.

Chapter 16: E-mailing Pictures

NOTE: Text-only email messages are similar to letters sent via US Mail. They don't take up much space in an email box. Pictures sent by email are like packages sent via US Mail. Pictures can take up a significant amount of space in an email box.

The size of an email message is more likely to be a problem when sending multiple pictures, although a single good quality picture can easily reach several megabytes in size. Earlier, we suggested that you use lower megapixel digital cameras for emailing. This recommendation was made because smaller pictures are generally better for emailing.

Viewing Attachment Size

After you have attached your picture, but before you send your email, look at the picture size shown on the attachment line. The picture size is displayed immediately after the picture title. Picture sizes are circled in the illustration shown below.

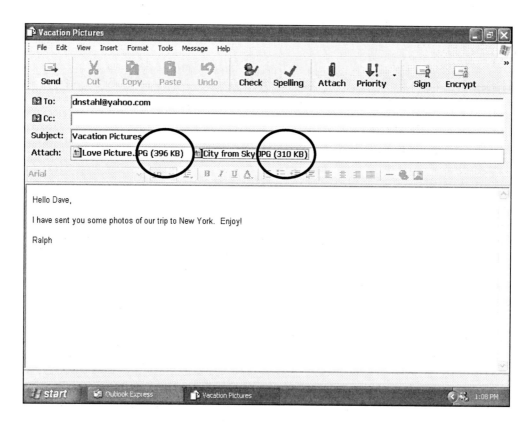

Notice that in the screen shot there are two pictures attached. The file sizes are 396KB and 310KB. You will typically have sizes indicated by two sets of initials, KB and MB. KB is short for kilobytes; MB is short for megabytes. The difference is important because KB is equal to 1000 bytes, and MB is equal to one million bytes.

KB=Kilobyte
KB=1000 Bytes
MB=Megabyte
MB=1,000,000 Bytes

What does this mean to you when you send pictures by email? As a rule of thumb, sending email attachments measured in KB's is OK because the size can be accommodated by most email services.

However, caution should be exercised when email attachment sizes reach the MB range. Some email systems may be unable to send or receive email messages that are 3+ megabytes.

Taking into account the maximum size of most email boxes, an attachment of approximately 3 megabytes is the largest you should send in a single email. Most, but not all, digital pictures will be below that size. However, if you do send a send a picture larger than 3 megabytes, your picture may not be delivered.

Important Points to Remember about Attachments:
- A picture or additional file sent through email it is called an attachment.
- Any type of computer file can be attached and emailed. Documents, spreadsheets, flyers, slideshows, music files, and picture files can all be attached to an email.
- These files are named attachments because they are normally copied from your computer, "attached" to an e-mail message, and then sent.
- Sending an attachment will NOT remove the original file from your computer. You are simply sending a copy.

- Knowing the total size of the email message, including your attachments, is important because excessively large emails may not be received by the intended recipients.

Receiving or Viewing Attachments

If you used email in the past and viewed pictures that someone sent you, you received an attachment. The person who composed the message attached a picture file from his or her computer and sent it to you, along with a standard email message.

Receiving an Emailed Picture Attachment: Step-by-Step Instructions

1. **Open your email.**
2. **Click once on INBOX.**
3. **Double click on the Subject line of the message to open the message.**
4. **Maximize the window if necessary.**
5. **Double click on the attachment name to open it.**
   - **The picture will open so it can be viewed.**
6. **Close the window using the "X" in the upper right corner when you are finished looking at the picture.**

Receiving an Emailed Picture Attachment: Visual Guide

Step One: Open your email, as you would normally.

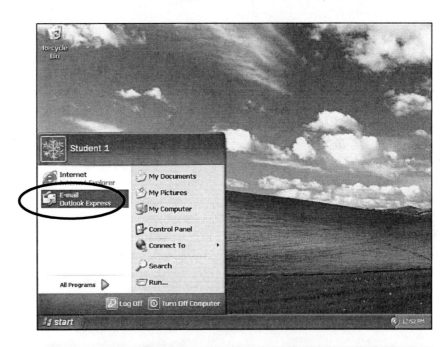

Step Two: Click once on INBOX.

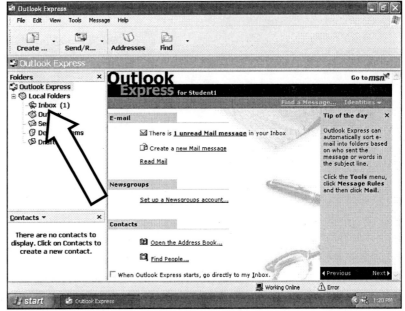

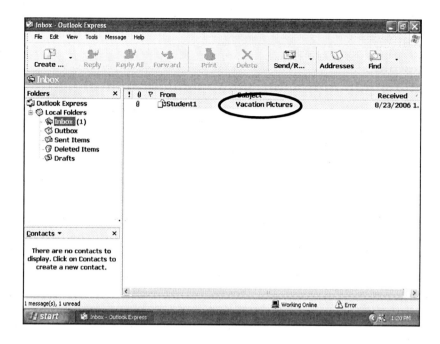

**Step Three:
Double click
on the
Subject line
of the
message to
open the
message.**

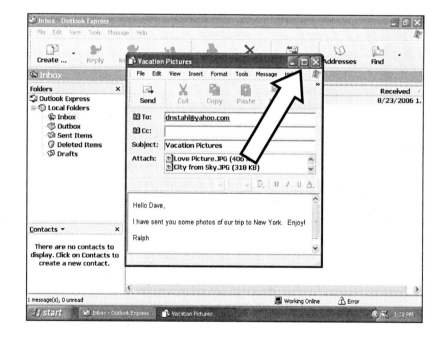

**Step Four:
Maximize the
window, if
necessary.**

Step Five:
Double click on
the attachment
name to open
it.

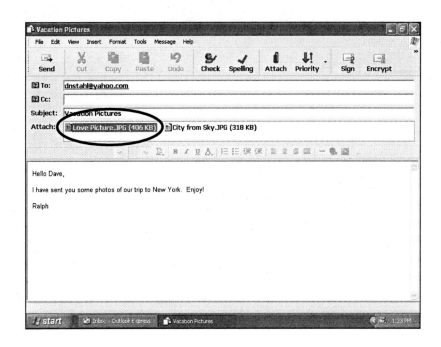

Step 5A:
The picture will
open so it can be
viewed.

Step Six:
When you are
finished looking
at the picture,
close the window
using the "X" in
the upper right
corner.

Problems Opening an Attachment

It is important to recognize that, although any type of file can be emailed, not every type of file can be viewed by the individual receiving the message. The emailed attachment can be viewed only if the person receiving the file has a program that can read the attached file.

This usually isn't a problem for picture attachments because most computers have a designated program to "read" or view picture files. Even basic computers with limited features have a program to read common picture files. You will learn to use this program, *Windows Picture and Fax Viewer*, in the next chapter.

If your computer cannot open or read a picture or file, it means the emailed file was created in a program that doesn't exist on the recipient's computer. For instance, if you email a spreadsheet attachment created in Microsoft Excel to a person who does not have the Microsoft Excel program, he or she generally will not be able to open and view the attachment.

All attachments look the same on your email screen. When you double-click on a readable attachment, the picture or file is opens and is displayed as sent. However, when you double click on an unreadable file, a new *"Open With"* window will appear, indicating that you do not have the ability to open the attachment.

This is what the recipient sees when the computer is unable to read an attachment:

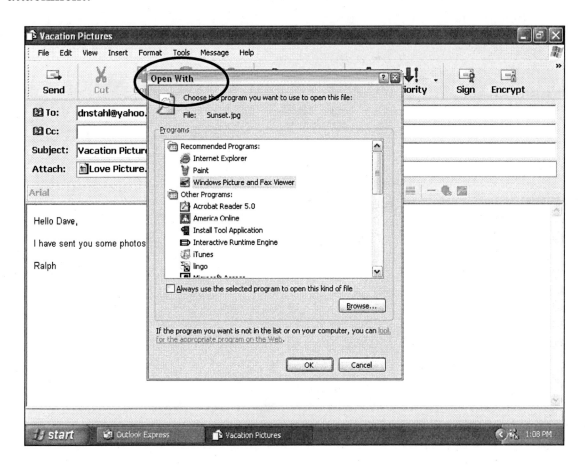

Did I Do Something Wrong?

It is often misconstrued that either the sender, or the recipient, of the email has done something wrong when an attachment cannot be viewed or when the *Open With* window appears. Don't worry, you have done nothing wrong. Usually, it is simply a case of the sender emailing a file created using a software program that isn't on the recipient's computer.

What Can I Do if I Cannot Open an Attachment?

If the attachment name includes an *extension* (the 3 or 4 letters at the end of the name, after the period) of .jpg, .gif, .bmp, or .tiff, you may be able to open it by using Windows Picture and Fax Viewer.

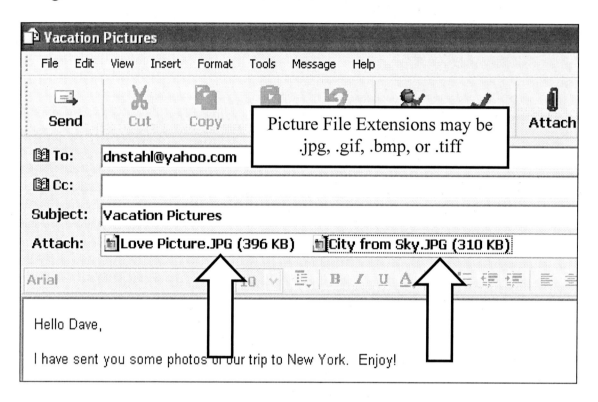

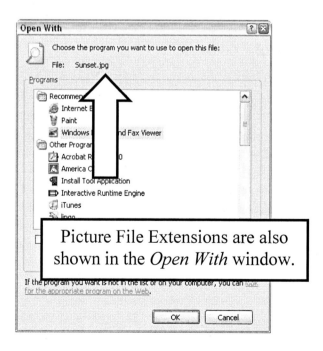

Opening a Picture Using the "Open With" Window: Step-by-Step Instructions

1. In the "Open With" box, click once on the WINDOWS PICTURE AND FAX VIEWER option from the list.
2. Click once on the OK button.
3. The picture will open in Window Picture and Fax Viewer.

Opening a Picture Using the "Open With" Window: Visual Guide

Step One: Click once on the WINDOWS PICTURE AND FAX VIEWER option.

**Step Two:
Click once on
the OK button.**

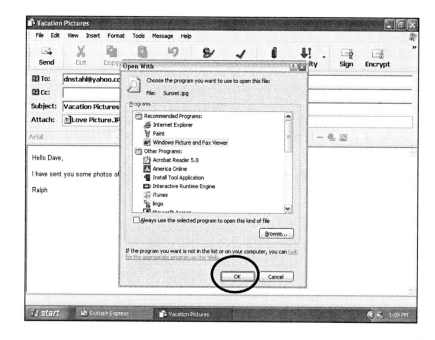

**Step Three:
The picture will
open in Window
Picture and Fax
Viewer.**

Non-Picture Attachments

If the file is not a picture, and doesn't have one of the aforementioned file extensions, it is best not to select a program to open the file. Even though the first direction asks you to "choose the program you want to use," do not try to read the file. Rather, you should close the window using the CANCEL button in the bottom right portion of the window.

If you try to open the file in a non-compatible program, the attachment may be damaged and will open in gibberish. If it is damaged, you will not be able to open the file later using the correct program. It is better to not attempt to open it. Instead, notify the person who sent you the attachment that you could not open it and ask what program was used to create the file.

If the file is not a picture, and does not have one of the specified file extensions, do not try to open the file.

Click CANCEL to close the window.

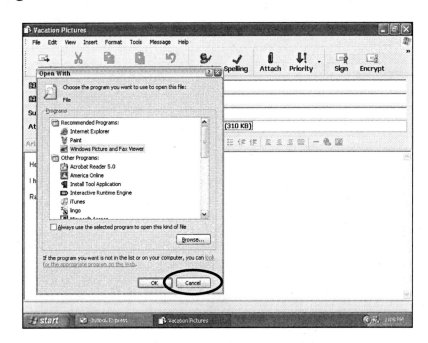

When a file attachment has been emailed in a program the recipient doesn't have, and the recipient cannot view it, there are only two only solutions:

1. The sender can recreate the file in a program the recipient possesses.
2. The recipient can get the necessary software to read the file. This is only a good option if you intend to read this type of file on a regular basis. Purchasing software to read a single file is expensive and usually not worth the cost.

Chapter 16: E-mailing Pictures

Chapter 17

Using Windows Picture and Fax Viewer

What You Will Learn in This Chapter:
- ✓ Understanding Windows Picture and Fax Viewer
- ✓ Viewing pictures using Windows Picture and Fax Viewer
- ✓ Viewing a slideshow in Windows Picture and Fax Viewer
- ✓ Printing pictures using Windows Picture and Fax Viewer

Section 37: Windows Picture and Fax Viewer

Windows Picture and Fax Viewer is included on most computers. The program allows you to (you guessed it!) view pictures and faxes. This section will focus on viewing pictures. Windows Picture and Fax Viewer opens automatically when you open a picture in the My Pictures folder.

You have accessed the program a few times already, simply by double-clicking on a picture file. The computer automatically "assigns" this program to open and display any picture files you save or receive. The assignments are made using the file extensions described earlier.

It is important to understand how to use some of the features in the Windows Picture and Fax Viewer because, if you don't have a photo editing program, you may need it to view pictures. You may also use Windows Picture and Fax Viewer to print pictures, display your pictures in a slideshow, or even save a copy of a picture.

Since the program is only a viewer, it is not ideal for editing pictures. The features, such as zoom and rotate, are viewing enhancements and are not ideal for making permanent changes to a picture.

Besides displaying pictures, Windows Picture and Fax Viewer allows you to:
- ✓ Scroll through pictures in a folder
- ✓ Print pictures, specific to size and color
- ✓ Save a copy of a picture
- ✓ Increase or decrease the picture preview size (zoom)
- ✓ View the picture in full size or as it best fits your window
- ✓ View a slide show of all of your pictures
- ✓ Open the pictures in an editing program. Note that, if you choose this option, it will automatically close the Windows Picture and Fax Viewer.

Here is a picture displayed in the Windows Picture and Fax

Windows Picture and Fax Viewer Toolbar

When the program is open, you will see a line of icons along the bottom of the picture. This is known as the toolbar. These icons represent all of the functions you can perform in the Windows Picture and Fax Viewer program.

Overview of the Windows Picture and Fax Viewer Toolbar

Previous Image: Returns to the previous picture in this folder.

Next Image: Moves to the next picture in this folder.

Best Fit: Reduces or enlarges the picture to fit to the window's current size.

Actual Size: Displays the picture without scaling.

Start Slide Show: Displays each picture in the folder in a slide show manner. Start, pause, navigate, or end the slide show using the slide show toolbar in the upper right corner.

Zoom In: Enlarges the displayed picture to twice its size.

Zoom Out: Reduces the displayed picture by half its size.

Rotate Clockwise: Rotates the picture by 90 degrees clockwise.

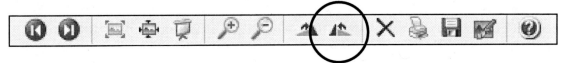

Rotate counter-clockwise: Rotates the picture by 90 degrees counter-clockwise.

Delete Image: Deletes the picture. Windows prompts you to confirm that you want to delete the picture. If you click *Yes*, the picture is deleted, and the next picture in the folder is displayed.

Print: Prints the current picture.

Copy To: Copies the picture file to another location. (Save a Copy)

Open for Editing: Opens the current picture in a photo editing program.

Help: Displays the Windows Picture and Fax Viewer Help file.

Using Features in Windows Picture and Fax Viewer

Chapter 17: Using Windows Picture and Fax Viewer

There are a few features in the Windows Picture and Fax Viewer that are especially useful for browsing and sharing pictures. In the next section, you will walk through the steps to print pictures, view a slideshow of your pictures, and set up a picture as your desktop background, all using Windows Picture and Fax Viewer.

Keep in mind that, although you have already learned these steps using the Picassa program, some readers may not have the Picassa program, or you may not always have access to Picassa. In either case, Windows Picture and Fax Viewer is available to perform these functions.

Printing Pictures from the Windows Picture and Fax Viewer

If you do not have Picassa or a similar program, you may choose to print directly from the My Documents folder.

Remember, all pictures transferred and saved to your computer have at least one copy in the My Pictures folder. To begin, you must access and open the pictures you have stored in the My Pictures folder.

Reviewing How to Access the My Pictures Folder and open a picture:

1. **Click on START.**
2. **Move the cursor to the My Pictures folder in the upper right portion of the start menu.**
3. **Click once with the left mouse button on MY PICTURES.**
4. **Double-click on the icon of the picture you want to open. The picture will open in Windows Picture and Fax Viewer.**

NOTE: The default program used to view pictures on your computer is Windows Picture and Fax Viewer. You should see the title "Windows Picture and Fax Viewer" in the blue title bar at the top of the window.

When the picture is open in Windows Picture and Fax Viewer, you should notice a line of small icons along the bottom of the picture. These icons allow you to perform specific functions with the picture you are viewing.

Chapter 17: Using Windows Picture and Fax Viewer

Within the display of icons, you will see an icon representing a printer (circled).

Printing Pictures Using Windows Picture and Fax Viewer: Step-by-Step Instructions

1. When Windows Picture and Fax Viewer is open, click once on the printer icon to begin the printing process.
   - A window titled Photo Printing *Wizard* will appear at the top of your current open window. A *wizard* is a program that walks you through the steps to complete a task. The window that appears first is simply a welcome screen, informing you that the wizard can help you print pictures.
2. Click the NEXT button with your left mouse button.
   a. This window displays all of the pictures in the folder you are currently viewing. In this example, it displays all the pictures in the My Pictures folder.
   b. There is a small green checkmark in the upper right corner of the picture you selected to print. This tells you that only this one picture has been selected to be printed.
      - It is possible to select more than one picture to print. To select another picture:
        1. Move your cursor to the checkbox located at the upper right corner of the picture.
        2. Position the tip of the cursor on the center of the checkbox.
        3. Click once with the left mouse button.
        4. This will insert a checkmark in the selected picture, indicating it should also be printed.
      - In this example, you will print only one picture.
3. Click the NEXT button with your left mouse button.
   a. This window helps you select the printer you want to use to print pictures. In most cases, home computer users will have only one printer installed.
   b. The name of the printer will appear in the box under the text "What printer would you like to use?"
      - If the wrong printer name appears in the box, select another printer by clicking directly on the printer

name. A drop down box will appear. Click on the name of the printer you want to use.

4. Click the NEXT button with your left mouse button.

    a. This window allows you to select the size of the picture you wish to print. Scroll down to view the various picture sizes. Select the desired picture size by clicking on it from the list.

    b. Select the number of copies you want to print by using the up/down arrows located next to "number of times to use each picture."

5. Click the NEXT button to complete the print setup.

    • The printing will automatically begin.

6. Click the FINISH button to complete the process and close the window.

Printing Pictures Using Windows Picture and Fax Viewer: Visual Guide

Step One: Click once on the printer icon to begin the printing process.

Step Two:
Click the NEXT button with your left mouse button.

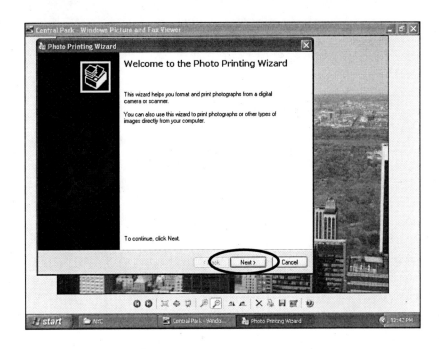

Step 2B:
Notice the small green checkmark.

This checkmark indicates that only this picture is selected to be printed.

Step Three:
Click the NEXT button with your left mouse button.

Step 3A:
If the wrong printer name appears in the box, select another printer by clicking on the printer name and selecting the correct printer from the drop down box.

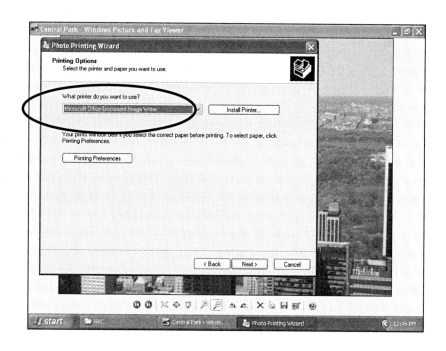

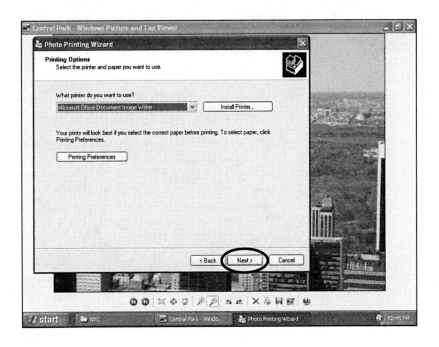

Step Four:
Click the NEXT
button.

Step 4A
Scroll down to
select the picture
size you want.

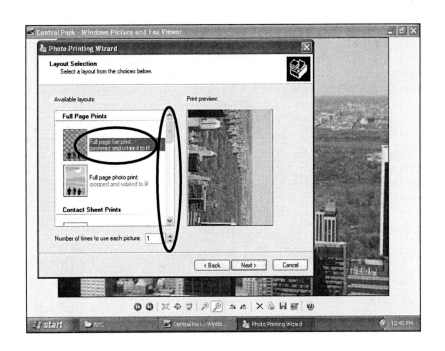

Step 4B
Select the
number of
copies you want
to print using
the up/down
arrows.

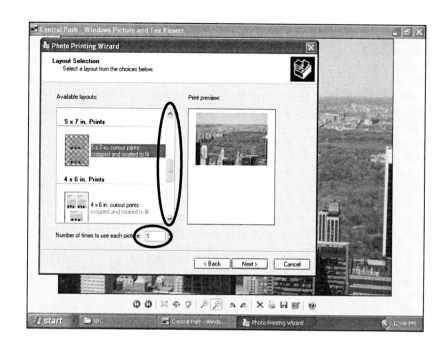

Step Five:
Click the
NEXT button
to complete the
print setup.

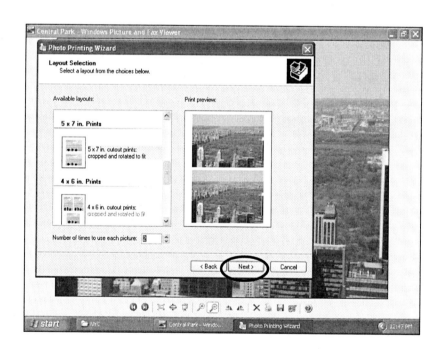

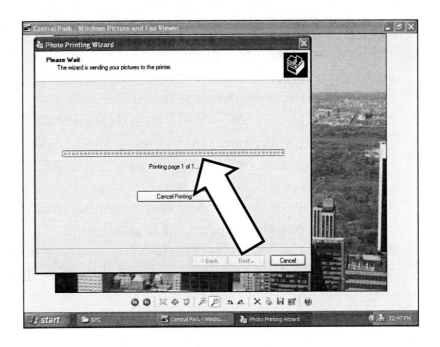

The printing status bar will appear letting you know the picture is being printed.

Step Six: Click the FINISH button to complete the process and close the window.

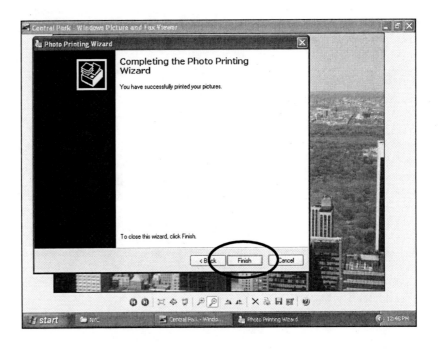

You have now completed the printing process using Windows Picture and Fax Viewer. Great job!

Chapter 17: Using Windows Picture and Fax Viewer

Viewing Pictures as a Slideshow Using Windows Picture and Fax Viewer: Step-by-Step Instructions

1. In the My Pictures Folder, double click to open a picture. This picture will start the slideshow.
2. Click on the VIEW AS SLIDESHOW icon on the toolbar.
    * The slideshow will begin.
    * The slides will automatically advance to the next picture every 5 seconds.
3. Move your mouse around the screen so that the control bar appears in the upper right corner of the slideshow.
4. Click on the "X" to return to Windows Picture and Fax Viewer.
    * You will be returned to the slideshow's starting picture.

Viewing Pictures as a Slideshow (Using Windows Picture and Fax Viewer): Visual Guide

Step One:
Open a picture.
This picture will
start the
slideshow.

**Step Two:
Click the VIEW
AS
SLIDESHOW
icon on the
toolbar.**

**The slideshow
will begin.**

The slideshow will automatically advance to the next picture every 5 seconds.

Step Three: Move your mouse around the screen so that the control bar appears in the upper right corner of the slideshow.

Step Four:
Click on the "X"
to return to
Windows
Picture and Fax
Viewer.

You will be
returned to the
starting picture
in the slideshow.

Now you know how to display and view all of your pictures in a slideshow.
Good job!

Changing the Background Picture (Using Windows Picture and Fax Viewer): Step-by-Step Instructions

1. In the My Pictures Folder, double click to open a picture.
2. The picture will be displayed in Windows Picture and Fax Viewer.
3. Right-click on the center of the picture.
    a. A right-click is a single click with the right mouse button.
    b. A shortcut menu will appear.
4. Click once on the SET AS DESKTOP BACKGROUND option.
5. Close all windows using the "X" in the upper, right corner. You will now be able to see your new background.

Changing the Background Picture (Using Windows Picture and Fax Viewer): Visual Guide

**Step One:
In the My
Pictures
Folder, double
click to open a
picture.**

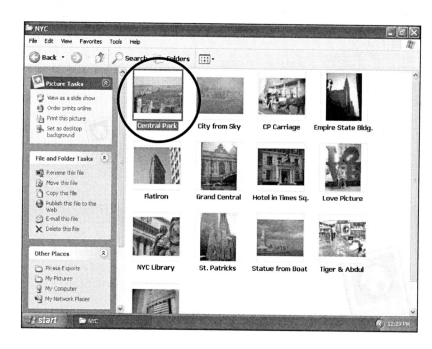

Step Two:
The picture
will be
displayed in
Windows
Picture and
Fax Viewer.

Step Three:
Right-click on
the center of
the picture.

A shortcut
menu will
appear.

Step Four:
Click once on the
SET AS
DESKTOP
BACKGROUND
option.

Step Five:
Close all
windows using
the "X" in the
upper right
corner.

You will now be able to see your new background.

You've come a long way! Remember to keep taking pictures and practicing the transfer, edit, and organization of your pictures. Before you know it, you'll be a picture pro, and will never need a film processor again!

We hope you enjoyed the book. Thanks so much!

Appendix!

Thank you for using the Web Wise Seniors' Digital Cameras for Beginners book. We hope you enjoyed learning with it. Please let us know what you think of the book. If you found it easy to use and enjoyed the learning experience, please tell your family and friends.

Feel free to send your comments and feedback
to us at the following address:

**Web Wise Seniors, Inc.
305 Woodstock Rd.
Eastlake, Ohio 44095**

Or Email us at
Larry@WebWiseSeniors.com

Thank You!

Appendix!

Web Wise Seniors is Proud to Present...
Basic Computer Manuals for Beginners

These books are the absolute best instruction manuals for beginners. WWS answers all of the questions asked by real students in our classes. Take a computer class home with you. Each manual is fully illustrated, providing step-by-step instructions in both written and picture format. Order your copy today!

BASIC COMPUTERS FOR BEGINNERS
Topics include:

- The Parts of the Computer
- How to use the Mouse
- Opening a Program using the Start Menu
- Turning the Computer On
- Saving Items
- Creating Folders
- Emptying the Recycle Bin
- Installing New Programs
- Using the Control Panel and Much More!!!!!!

BASIC WORD FOR BEGINNERS
Topics include:

- The Basics
- Short-cuts/Tricks
- Adding Pictures and Borders
- Cutting and Pasting
- Creating Columns
- Mail Merge
- Margins
- Printing
- Problem Solving and Much More!!!!!!

To Order Call Toll Free: 1-866-232-7032

Appendix!

Web Wise Seniors is Proud to Present...
Basic Computer Manuals for Beginners

THE INTERNET FOR BEGINNERS
Topics include:
- What can you Find on the Internet
- Selecting the Internet Service that's Right for You
- Comparing Cable, DSL and Dial-up
- Homepages and how to Change Them
- Understanding Browsers
- Using Web Addresses
- Surfing with Hyperlinks
- Search Engines
- Creating a Favorites List
- And Much More…

EMAIL FOR BEGINNERS
Topics include:
- Selecting the Email Service that's Right for You
- What makes up an Email Address
- Avoiding Viruses & Junk Mail
- Sending Emails
- Forwarding Emails
- Reply vs. Reply All
- Keeping an Address Book
- Sending Attachments
- Opening Attachments
- And Much More…

To Order Call Toll Free: 1-866-232-7032

Appendix!

Web Wise Seniors is Proud to Present...
Basic Computer Manuals for Beginners

EXCEL FOR BEGINNERS

Excel for Beginners introduces the many uses of spreadsheets in the home and at work. Readers will learn how to create working budgets and interactive lists while mastering the skills needed to take their abilities in Excel to the next level. Essential topics such as sequencing, sorting, formatting, freezing, and repeating will be discussed, and much more!!!!!!

OUTLOOK FOR BEGINNERS

Outlook for Beginners will help you throw away all of those yellow sticky notes and organize yourself like never before. Outlook will help you keep track of your busy schedule at home and at work. Don't get lost in the hustle and bustle of life. Readers will learn how to record important contact information, schedule meetings, send email and manage to-do lists.

To Order Call Toll Free: 1-866-232-7032

Appendix!

Web Wise Seniors is Proud to Present...
Basic Computer Manuals for Beginners

ACCESS FOR BEGINNERS

Access for Beginners will take the fear and complexity out of databases. Readers will learn the power of databases and the steps to build their own databases from scratch. Whether its mailing lists, personal cataloguing, or organizing business transactions, Access for Beginners is the place to start.

POWERPOINT FOR BEGINNERS

PowerPoint for Beginners covers the basic skills needed to put together a professional quality slide show. Starting from the basics, readers will learn how to control their views, add & delete slides, insert exciting animations, develop smooth slide transitions, and much more!!!

To Order Call Toll Free: 1-866-232-7032

Appendix!

Notes: